Spinning Tails

Spinning Tails

Helicopter Stories

Jan Hornung

iUniverse, Inc.
New York Lincoln Shanghai

Spinning Tails
Helicopter Stories

All Rights Reserved © 2003 by Janine Hornung

iUniverse, Inc.

For information address:
iUniverse, Inc.
2021 Pine Lake Road, Suite 100
Lincoln, NE 68512
www.iuniverse.com

All material is printed or reprinted here with permission from each author as noted.

ISBN: 0-595-30221-1

Printed in the United States of America

To all who have known the joy and sorrow of helicopter flight.

As always, to Skyler: You are my wings.

When once you have tasted flight,
you will forever walk the earth
with your eyes turned skyward,
for there you have been,
and there you will always long to return.

Leonardo da Vinci, 1452-1519

CONTENTS
(THE FLIGHT PLAN)

FOREWORD

The helicopter is probably the most versatile
instrument ever invented by man.
It approaches closer than any other vehicle
to fulfillment of mankind's ancient dreams
of the flying horse and the magic carpet.

Igor Sikorsky, 1889–1972

PREFACE
(PREFLIGHT)

I realize that there are no "helicopter stories,"
just stories of men and women whose lives were changed
by the places that helicopters led them or allowed them to go.

Bob Mackey
Dustoff pilot
RVN 1969–1970

ACKNOWLEDGEMENTS
(CREW ROSTER)

A Special Thank You to:

- ∞ Ruth Hay—for her excellent editing abilities and to Hal Hay for uploading and downloading hundreds of computer files for this task, two of the most beautiful people I know. Because of you, I fly.
- ∞ Pat Hewatt—for her support, her friendship, her amusing e-mails, and of course, her beautiful poetry.
- ∞ Deanna Gail Shlee Hopkins—for her friendship and all she does for so many.
- ∞ Bill McDonald—a spiritual warrior, for his friendship and for his stories, and for giving me the honor of being his editor.
- ∞ Gary Jacobson—for his entertaining e-mails and for sharing his wonderful story and poem for this book.
- ∞ Mike Subritzky—the Kiwi Kipling who gives so much to so many, for sharing his talents.
- ∞ My good friends Ken Melusky and Slim Myers, both incredible men, for sharing their stories.
- ∞ Janis Nark—an amazing woman, for sharing one of her stories.
- ∞ Patty Biegun—a woman whose beauty and insight shines through in her stories, for bringing me into her life as her editor.
- ∞ Del "Abe" Jones—for his poems that put the world in perspective for me.
- ∞ Pat Kenny—for living his dream and encouraging me.
- ∞ Each of these wonderful writers and poets I came to know and admire through their stories, poems, insights and personal e-mails as they shared a piece of their lives and a part of their souls. Thank you to: Ron Bower, Rodney R. Brown, Sharon Vander Ven Cummings, James Dunbar, Galen Foster, Larry Harty, James M. Hopkins, Johnny Hutcherson, Larry Kimmith, Ron Leonard, Bob Mackey, Bobby McBride, John Moller, Tom Nesbitt, Anthony Pahl, Jim Schueckler, and Mary A. Smith.

INTRODUCTION
(TAKEOFF)

"**Thank you**" to everyone who wrote stories and poems for this book. I regret I could not use all of them. Of the hundreds of wonderful writings I received, I chose the "editor's favorites" to present here.

From the jungles of Vietnam to the heavens of Hawaii, across the world from New Zealand to America, and around-the-world flights, you'll fly along with the pilots, crew members, soldiers, Donut Dollies, nurses, and adventure seekers.

Join Huey 091 in her journey from Vietnam to a backyard wedding decades later. Share the anxiety of a wartime helicopter crew lost in the fog over the jungle. Find out why some people dream of helicopter flight, while others have nightmares of the memories.

Laugh along with flight follies, admire the unsung heroes of the flight line, scream as you crash into another helicopter in midair, and put those in-flight emergency procedures to work when you hear, "You're on Fire!"

More than three dozen writers contributed stories, poems, quips, and insights to *Spinning Tails*. These represent just a few of the myriad adventures, heartaches, ecstasies, horrors, and wonders that helicopters have to offer. You'll also learn a bit of helicopter history, winged wisdom, and flight facts scattered throughout the book.

Strap in, hang on, and get ready for the flight of your life.

"Tower, *Spinning Tails* ready for takeoff."

Jan Hornung
Angels in Vietnam: Women Who Served
KISS the Sky: Helicopter Tales
This is the Truth As Far As I Know, I Could Be Wrong

CHAPTER 1

Flight Follies

It is far easier to start something than it is to finish it.

Amelia Earhart, 1897-1937

Winged Wisdom

ও Let children know they can do anything
they want to do—even fly.

Around the World

Flying around the world in a helicopter is like raising kids. When you've finally figured out how to do it the right way, you've finished.
✦ Ron Bower

Ron Bower set the around-the-world speed record in 1996 when he flew a Bell 430 westbound around the world in 17 days and 6 hours. He also holds the eastbound around-the-world record in a helicopter, which he flew solo in a Bell 206B Jet Ranger in 1994 in 24 days and 4 hours.

For more about Ron Bower and his company, Bower Helicopter, Inc., go online to http://www.bowerhelicopter.com

📖

Winged Wisdom

     ೞ Take time to appreciate the scenery.
     ೞ Don't be afraid to ask for help.
    ೞ You'll never run out of fuel at an inconvenient time
if you take the winds into consideration.

Little Green Bugs

My first day as a helicopter pilot in Vietnam, probably January 10, 1969, I was assigned as Peter Pilot to one of the most experienced aircraft commanders.

Everything was going just like flight school: quick briefing, mark our maps, write down frequencies, preflight the aircraft. Just like flight school. Crank up the birds, pick up the grunts, take off in formation, head for the landing zone, the LZ.

On final approach, the Aircraft Commander took the controls and said, "Stay on the controls with me, but I will do the flying, understand? OK, you've got it."

Just like flight school, I think to myself.

Some noise and smoke in the LZ; we dropped off the grunts. Neat! Just like flight school. Just like I expected.

After the formation was back at cruising altitude, I asked the Aircraft Commander about the one thing that I hadn't seen in flight school. "What were those little green bugs?"

"What little green bugs?"

"When we were on final, and down there in the LZ, there were little green bugs."

"Are you kidding me?"

"No, there were a whole lot of little green bugs, and they were going real fast."

"You must be kidding me."

"No, they were there, real fast and real straight."

"Those were tracers."

"Tracers!?! But they were coming toward us!"

"Yes, they were coming toward us!"

"Do you mean they were shooting at us?"

"Yes, they were shooting at us," he replied smugly.

"Oh," said I, the humble newbie.

About 30 minutes later, while we were refueling, the crew chief said on the intercom, "Sir, I think we better shut down to see how much damage we have; some of those little green bugs bit us back here (snicker)."

✦ By Jim Schueckler

Jim Schueckler was a 21-year-old helicopter pilot with the 192nd Assault Helicopter Company, Phan Thiet, 1969–1970. He is "still married to the same wonderful woman who saw me off to war." Jim and his wife, Judy, have "three children and two cute grandkids."

Schueckler is founder and webmaster of the original virtual wall, *The Virtual Wall, Vietnam Veterans Memorial* at http://www.VirtualWall.org

"Since March 1997, *The Virtual Wall* has honored the 58,220 men and women named on the Vietnam Veterans' Memorial, those who gave the ultimate sacrifice. Each name or photo on our index page links to a personal memorial, either on this site or on personal web sites elsewhere." ✛ Jim Schueckler

Jim Schueckler's story "The Day It Snowed In Vietnam" is published in *Angels in Vietnam: Women Who Served*.

📖

Winged Wisdom

℅ If you don't know where you are,
you can't figure out where you're going.
℅ If you don't know where you're going,
all the flight plans and aerial maps in the world won't help you.

The First Unofficial Bombing Raid of Cambodia

The day began with a short briefing in flight operations. Normally, I would be on the flight line waiting with my ship. This day's mission, however, was different because we were carrying men into an area that looked like Cambodia on the map. I was told that we were going to take a small group of men on a single-ship mission to grid coordinates such and such.

When I looked at where that was on the map, I blurted out something about that being in the Parrot's Beak, inside of Cambodia. The two pilots glared at me and stated once again that we were going to grid coordinates such and such. I restated the obvious, and they told me for the last time that we were heading to those grid coordinates and any mention of Cambodia was to be forgotten.

We gathered our gear and loaded the chopper. We did a thorough preflight inspection and lifted off just as the sun was rising over the tops of the surrounding jungle around Phu Loi. We pulled the Huey up and into the morning sunrise. I always loved flying that time of the day. Sunrise in Vietnam with all the haze made for some beautiful colors in the early morning skies, and also at sunset.

We went to a small base camp close to the border between Vietnam and Cambodia and picked up a group of men wearing an assortment of unidentifiable uniforms. No one had anything that would label them as American or even NATO. They were on some kind of secret mission and their nationalities were purposely disguised. They also had weapons from eastern block countries, AK-47s and such. These guys did not talk at all. Their conversations were nonexistent and there were no smiles. These six men that we were taking to those grid coordinates were all business.

We flew to the grid coordinates at a high altitude. I was used to flying most of our missions at treetop level or even lower at times, but on this mission we were up about as high as I have ever flown in a helicopter in Vietnam. When we got close to the grid coordinates of the LZ, we began a steep dive and cruised into the LZ just above the treetops from about two miles out. I had my M-60 at the ready, but the jungle was so thick I couldn't even see the ground under the trees, let alone any VC or NVA who might be taking some shots at us. I could feel the tension of my passengers the closer we got.

All of a sudden we sprang upon a clear opening just big enough for our ship to touch down and take off again. It was a tight fit, but it was the only opening in the jungle for miles in either direction. We quickly dropped down into the LZ. The landing was not very soft as we slightly bounced. The men were off before the Huey had even stopped sliding forward on the ground. I gave the pilots the okay to take off. Without any hesitation, they were trying to get out of there as fast as they could. We barely cleared the treetops as the pilot pulled the collective throttle up and began heading back to get supplies for these men.

The good news was that the LZ was cold (no enemy fire). Our concern, however, was that we not attract too much attention because we had to go back there again with more supplies. The possibility of having a hot LZ increased the more times we kept landing in it.

We went back to where we had originally picked up the men, and we took on a full load of supplies of ammo, c-rations, medical supplies, and for some strange reason, two cases of toilet paper.

It was a long and boring flight back to the LZ at grid coordinates such and such. I was actually getting sleepy and was having trouble staying awake. I began to look at the cases of toilet paper and wondered what one roll would look like if I threw it out from 6,000 feet. I was wondering if it would unwind and stretch out to its full length. So, I decided to solve this personal mystery. I opened one of the cases and removed one roll for my airborne experiment over the jungle of Cambodia.

I pulled about six feet of it from the roll to get it started. I then tossed it straight out of my helicopter into the sky. It began to unravel immediately. I am not sure how long a roll of classic American-made soft toilet paper is, but within a few seconds that entire roll was floating like paper fireworks slowly onto the tops of the triple-canopy jungle below me. In fact, it looked so neat, and I was so bored, that I decided to throw another roll. Well, one good thing led to another, and by the time we had almost gotten to the LZ to unload the supplies, one of the cases of toilet paper was totally empty. So, I decided to drop that "cardboard bomb" overboard to join the toilet paper. I did not want to have an empty box show up in the LZ.

The LZ proved to be uneventfully safe, and we were able to successfully unload everything quickly and leave right away. We pulled back up to 6,000 feet, so we had a great view of the entire area below us for miles. All of a sudden, I heard one of the pilots yelling at me about what he was seeing.

"Mac, what in the hell is all that white crap over the tops of the jungle?"

"It almost appears to look like someone toilet-papered the jungle tops. Is that possible?" the other pilot added.

Of course, I was now caught red-handed, so I had to tell the truth.

"Yes, Sir, that sure looks like toilet paper to me also. We must have had a case fall out when we hit some air turbulence. I assume that all those rolls just popped out of the box and unraveled themselves across the tops of the jungle. Yep, that is what it looks like to me, Sir."

One of the pilots began to yell at me, but I detected a slight laughing sound from the other one or both.

"Mac, this was a classified mission into Cambodia where we are not supposed to be. Now you've bombed Cambodian territory with American toilet paper! It's spread out for miles on the tops of their jungle. Everyone will know we were here!"

"But, Sir, we are not in Cambodia, we are only in grid coordinates such and such," I replied.

There was a long silence. Then I heard, even over the sound of all the helicopter noise, the crew, including my left door gunner, laughing.

"Okay Mac, if you say the case fell out, then that is what the official report will say. In the meantime, let's pray for some good heavy rainfall to wash all the evidence of our 'bombing raid' away," one of the pilots said.

Thus ended the first unofficial bombing raid of Cambodia in 1967. Of course, it wasn't Cambodia, it was only grid coordinates such and such! And I swear that the box must have really fallen out. That is my story and I am sticking to it. If I tell you anymore, I will have to kill you!

✦ By Bill McDonald
128th Assault Helicopter Company, Phu Loi, South Vietnam
LZ Angel, http://www.lzangel.com
The Vietnam Experience, http://www.vietnamexp.com

"The First Unofficial Bombing Raid of Cambodia" is reprinted here, with permission, from Bill McDonald's book, *A Spiritual Warrior's Journey*.

Bill McDonald served in Vietnam from November 1966 through November 1967 as a crew chief/door gunner on a Huey UH-1D with the 128th Assault Helicopter Company, at Phu Loi Army Airfield.

"I was wounded, shot up, and shot down. I received several awards including the Distinguished Flying Cross, Bronze Star, Purple Heart, and 14 Air Medals.

"I got out of the Army and married my high school sweetheart, Carol. In January 2003, we celebrated 33 years of marriage. We have two grown children, a son and a daughter, and one very wonderful grandson born in 2000. My wife and I are still best friends. We both grew up in Sunnyvale, California, and we share the same friends who go all the way back to the first and second grades.

"I retired from the United States Postal Service, where I was a safety specialist. I now try to help veterans and their families deal with the aftermath of the Vietnam War through my Support Network on my web site, *The Vietnam Experience* at http://www.vietnamexp.com, a web site that shares the emotional and spiritual experiences of the Vietnam War through poetry, stories, art, and photos by combat veterans. The web site has had more than three million visitors as of the fall of 2003.

"In 2002, I was involved in the making of the documentary film *In the Shadow of the Blade* about the effects of the Huey helicopter in Vietnam. We flew a restored Huey helicopter more than 10,000 miles across this nation, and we listened to thousands of veterans and their families. It became a very spiritual and emotional journey for all of us on the crew and for those we were able to reach out and touch. The documentary film chronicles our flight and those we met along the way with wonderful music, interviews, and footage of the Huey in flight. The film had its premiere in Austin, Texas, on November 8, 2003, at the LBJ Presidential Library Auditorium. (See "A Huey Tail Come True," by Patty Biegun, chapter 11, for one of the amazing adventures of this helicopter.)

"I went back to Vietnam in the spring of 2002 and visited the location where I had been shot down and wounded in April of 1967. I was able to meet my former enemies and their families. It helped bring some peace and healing to that part of my life. Read about Huey 091 at *In the Shadow of the Blade*, http://www.intheshadowoftheblade.com

"These stories and others from my life are in my book, *A Spiritual Warrior's Journey*, http://www.lzangel.com/WarBook.htm, published November 2003."
✦ Bill McDonald

Bill McDonald's story about Martha Raye with photograph, "Colonel Maggie: Nurse, Entertainer, and Honorary Green Beret," along with some of his poetry is published in *Angels in Vietnam: Women Who Served*. See Bill McDonald's stories in this book: "All Washed Up in Georgia," chapter 1; "Answer to a Prayer," chapter 2; and "Life or Death Decision," chapter 7.

📖

Flight Facts: In war, a landing zone, LZ, under enemy fire is referred to as a "hot LZ." A "cold LZ" is not under enemy fire.

Winged Wisdom

  √ Something will always go wrong. Be ready for it.
  √ Looking good in a flight suit is important.

All Washed Up in Georgia

In the winter of 1967, I was stationed at Fort Benning, Georgia, fresh from the battlefields of South Vietnam. All I had wanted to do was to serve my last 11 months and get out of the Army. The new helicopter company that I was assigned to had only one functional Huey and an old surplus chopper from the Korean War. There were more than 200 other Vietnam veteran crew chiefs in this stateside aviation company, all serving out their enlisted time as I was. We were just more war surplus, kind of being stored out of the way. There was no real use for any of us, but the Army was going to hang onto us in case there was some national emergency. None of us were ever going to go back to Vietnam—we were all too short (time left in Army) for that. Worse yet, we all had a bad attitude about military life. Being old veterans, none of us gave a hoot for authority or stateside discipline. Finding something to keep us busy was the only real challenge for the career officers of the unit.

When I went to my new unit, I was faced with the grim prospect of some potentially fierce competition if I wanted to fly in order to keep my flight pay status. There was only one crew chief position, and all 200 plus of those veteran crew chiefs wanted it. For some reason, known only to God, I was assigned to the one and only Huey that they had, which was being used as a medical evacuation helicopter. It was an old Huey model, but it flew, and it sure beat hanging around the company policing up cigarette butts all day.

The duty required me to stay in the hangar area to receive any phone calls that might come in requesting us to medically evacuate someone. Almost everyday went by with no phone calls and no visitors. I slept on a foldout cot, and someone in a jeep brought my meals from the company mess hall. My 48-hour shifts included weekends. After a shift, I would come back to the company area, shower and change, go to the PX if I needed any personal items; then, I went back to standby in the hot and muggy old hangar, waiting for a mission.

If I got a mission, I was to immediately call the pilots at home. They would drive out to the airfield where I would have the ship serviced and ready to go. I was lucky if the pilots even kicked the skids and walked around the aircraft to inspect it. They more or less expected me to have as much of the preflight inspection done as possible without starting up the engines. They were very trusting. Had they realized how little confidence I had in my own abilities, they might have had some very scary thoughts about not checking it over better themselves. The key, however, was to get into the air and to the medical extraction LZ (landing zone) as soon as possible. It could be a life or death situation, but it usually was not.

One afternoon we got a call from a Special Forces training camp up on a hilltop in Tennessee. Seems some young sergeant had a gas-fueled camping lantern explode in his face. He needed to be evacuated to a hospital as soon as possible for the treatment of his burns. We were the quickest option since the sergeant and his unit were several miles out in a wilderness area that had no access roads. We were still many miles away, so we got the old bird up and headed north, pushing it for all the speed it could generate.

When we got to the LZ, it reminded me of Vietnam. They even had to cut out a small area of trees for us to land. It was almost dark when I loaded him onto the ship and headed back to Georgia. We dropped him off at the closest hospital and proceeded to the Atlanta Airport to get some much-needed fuel. We called the control tower and got permission to land next to several large fixed-wing civilian aircraft. We were instructed to wait there for a large fuel truck that would deliver our fuel.

Up on the second floor of the adjacent building was a large windowed wall. This was where people waited to board or to meet people coming off of the airlines. It afforded them a great view of the airfield as well. It seemed that our Army helicopter was attracting lots of attention. I saw a sea of faces watching us shut down on the tarmac. Seeing that I had an audience watching, I strutted around my helicopter, checking stuff and thinking I looked really cool. I had on my flight jacket and helmet, and I looked like the tough aviator warrior that I was. I could not help but notice that there were several young, very good-looking women waving at us through the windows. I, of course, waved back in a manly and macho way. After we refueled, the pilots said they wanted to walk around the airport to find hot coffee and food. That idea sounded good to me as well.

The fuel truck arrived to give us a full load of JP-4 jet fuel. I figured they would pump it for us, but the guy just pointed to the hose and motioned for me to do it myself. Now, I had never pumped gas from this big of a truck with the high-speed pumps that it used to fill large airliners. I had always been used to the very slow pumps on the Army trucks. I was used to taking the handle with one hand and just squeezing off several gallons a minute. I reached up and took the handle of the nozzle with one hand and put it in the gas-refueling hole of the Huey, which is just about head high on me. The guy in the truck turned on the pump, and that is when all hell broke loose.

I was trying to hold a tiger by the tail. That hose was pumping hundreds of gallons of jet fuel out faster than I had ever seen. It pulled me onto the ground and began to snake around the surface of the airfield with me hanging onto it. The fuel was shooting up and onto everything around me, including the truck, the helicopter, and myself. Finally, after what seemed like hours, he turned off the pump and the hose and I went limp. I saw an ocean of liquid all around me. I was sitting in a sea of highly flammable jet fuel.

I glanced up at the windows and could see that I was the center of everyone's attention. I wanted to hide and go away and die. I looked at my two pilots who were still strapped in their seats looking at me and the potential dangers. Then, I heard the sounds of fire trucks pulling up next to us.

The firemen pulled several hoses next to me and sprayed me with a fire-retardant foam, which in a few short seconds covered me from head to foot. They proceeded to spray off that with ice cold water. I was still standing, but as the seconds dragged by, I felt smaller and smaller. There was no place for me to hide. I knew eventually that I also had to get back into the helicopter and face the joking from my crew. Finally, they had washed me and everything else around me, and I was permitted to move.

I slowly got back into the helicopter, all cold and wet but more embarrassed than anything else. I did not look back up at the window area of the airport. I quickly closed the doors and we took off. The pilots decided to forget about getting any coffee or food, but they certainly didn't forget me. Sitting there all soaking wet and chilled, I didn't wish to spend any more time in Atlanta. Frankly, I just didn't give a damn!

✦ By Bill McDonald
  The Vietnam Experience, http://www.vietnamexp.com
  LZ Angel, http://www.lzangel.com

"All Washed Up In Georgia" is reprinted here, with permission, from Bill McDonald's book, *A Spiritual Warrior's Journey*.

📖

Winged Wisdom

                             ℞ Learn to listen more than you talk.
                    ℞ Learn to listen to several radios at once.
               ℞ Don't talk over someone else on the radio.
     ℞ You can sing in a helicopter, and the rest of the crew won't hear you.

A Failure to Communicate

I was a young first lieutenant in the Indiana National Guard flying the venerable UH-1H Huey. I was participating in Annual Training exercises at Camp Atterbury, Indiana.

My unit had received a command console and had installed it in one of our Hueys. The console was fairly large and took up most of the area behind the pilot seats where the jump seat is normally installed. The console consisted of several FM radio transmitter/receivers and included a multitude of knobs, volume controls, and toggle switches. The purpose of the console was to allow a field commander the ability to communicate with all of his elements on the ground in order to provide real time Command and Control. The console allowed several individuals to transmit and receive at the same time.

The antennas were wire elements that ran the length of the tail boom and were installed on both sides of the aircraft. Since this was a new piece of equipment, one of our missions for this AT (Annual Training) period was to give the console an in-flight shakedown. Unfortunately, the console had just recently been installed at the Flight Facility, and there had been no time for anyone to train on or become familiar with the equipment. As it turned out, the infantry brigade commander that we were supporting was aware that we had brought a "Command and Control" bird to AT with us, and he wanted to try it out personally.

Being the good platoon leader that I was, I had myself assigned to the mission. The brigade commander had been around a long time and had an extensive background working with aviation units. He had even been awarded his own personal flight helmet, which he had painted infantry blue. He arrived at the airfield along with his XO (executive officer) and his command sergeant major. They were given the standard preflight briefing and a short introduction on operation of the command console, as best we understood it. The crew chief got the three of them strapped in and hooked up as my copilot and I prepared to crank the Huey. Our mission was to fly wherever the brigade commander told us, while he and his XO navigated us around the 24,000-acre training reservation.

Elements of his brigade were scattered from one end of the reservation to the other. In the center of the reservation is a no-fly impact area that includes an air-to-ground gunnery range. The area was "hot" and full of artillery and Air Force zoomies. As we departed the airfield, the colonel and his onboard staff were paging through their CEOIs (Communications Electronics Operation Instructions) to obtain radio frequencies and unit call signs for the day. Operating a tactical aircraft in a high-intensity military training environment is a challenging task. It did not take us long to figure out that anytime anyone using the command console used his push-to-talk button, it cut out anyone else who needed to transmit, including the two pilots.

If you can imagine flying in an environment where the pilots are required to talk to ground, tower, in-route controllers, Range Control operations, and an air-to-ground gunnery tower, you can see that the radio plays an extremely important role. Talking with all of these agencies is required in order to safely traverse the training area.

Meanwhile, the ground commander and his staff in the back of the aircraft have the responsibility to communicate with selected ground units in order to coordinate their tactical moves. The console allows several individuals to transmit on different FM radios to different ground units. We found during the course of the "shakedown" flight that no more than one individual could transmit at the same time. I'm not certain if it was supposed to work that way, or if that was just the way it was installed.

So, the brigade commander was attempting to contact units at the same time the XO was trying to transmit, and all of these simultaneous radio transmissions were keeping the pilots from talking on their radios! After some minutes of playing "key the mike as quick as you can whenever there is a millisecond of dead air," I was able to get everyone's attention and provide some hastily developed rules. If the pilot needed to use the radio he would hold up his hand in plain view and everyone else would need to end their conversations as quickly as possible.

This worked reasonably well when all parties concerned were actually looking up and didn't have their faces buried in a CEOI. My copilot and I ascertained that we could fly the aircraft safely in the environment and play radio tag at the same time. Fortunately for us, there were not a lot of aircraft in the AO (area of operations) at that particular time, which allowed us to continue our mission.

The UH-1H, on a typical summer day with a light load, has about an hour and a half of mission time before fuel starts getting critical. We were about 45 minutes into the flight by now, and the commander and his XO had not been able to raise one ground unit on the command console. There were short acknowledgements that someone had heard an initial call, but no actual communications had occurred. Our crew chief, who had been listening to all of this, deduced that the antennas must be directional and would only work effectively when the ground unit was on the same side of the aircraft as the antenna.

Well, this was a great revelation to the colonel, who then directed us to orbit the aircraft, keeping the right side of the tail boom toward the ground unit whenever he was transmitting from the radios on the right side of the console, and to the left whenever the XO was transmitting from the radios on the left side of the console. We obviously complied with this request and began orbiting right or left based on whichever colonel was transmitting.

After another 40 minutes or so of this activity, it became painfully apparent that this approach was no more effective than our earlier attempts. The crew chief then deduced that the console must have been wired backwards and the right side antennas were connected to the left side radios and vise versa. The new directive was to orbit the aircraft keeping the ground unit on the left side of the aircraft whenever the brigade commander was transmitting from one of the right-side console radios and just the opposite for the XO on the left side. As the copilot navigated us to the next ground unit's grid coordinates, the colonel and his XO were flipping through the CEOI to ascertain call signs, challenges, and passwords.

Realizing that time was of the essence, the commander and his XO were keying their respective mike buttons as fast as they could, attempting to make contact with one of their units on the ground. I kept trying to break in on the intercom each time I heard dead air, but one of the dueling colonels would always manage to beat me. Finally in desperation, I turned both my and the copilot's intercom switches to the "private" position and announced that I would be landing at the colonel's TOC (Tactical Operations Center). The "private" position on the pilots' radio console allows the two pilots to talk discretely to each other and not interrupt radio transmissions from the rear.

I asked for a before-landing check, and began my descent into the small opening in the forest toward the orange panel marker that indicated the touchdown area. Just as the skids touched the ground, the brigade commander made contact with the first ground unit of the day and yelled into the intercom, "Dunbar, I think I've got this son of a bitch figured out!"

The copilot and I quickly exchanged glances, and in my best pilot voice, I informed the colonel that we were very close to a 20-minute fuel light and that the mission was over. He looked around in amazement, began unbuckling his seat belt, spewed an amazing string of expletives, and un-assed the aircraft. The flight back to the FARP (Forward Area Refueling Point) was quite uneventful and wonderfully quiet. I managed to keep myself away from that command console for the remainder of AT.

✦ By James M. Dunbar
   CW4, Army retired, 1980–2000, Master Aviator

James Dunbar began his military career as a corporal with the Marine Corps, then as a sergeant with the Air Force Reserves. He later transferred to the Army and attended OCS, Officer Candidate School, and flight school. He attained the rank of captain, then reverted to warrant officer, retiring as a chief warrant officer 4. During his aviation career, Dunbar flew UH-1 Hueys, OH-58 Scouts, and UH-60 Black Hawks with the Indiana National Guard.

He has been married to his "wonderfully patient and understanding wife, Mickey," since 1971. They have two sons, Jason and Jeff.

Read James Dunbar's story "Living the Dream," chapter 10.

📖

CHAPTER 2

Vietnam Flying

*What freedom lies in flying,
what God-like power it gives to men.*

Charles A. Lindbergh, 1902-1974

Airborne Stairs

We flew upon those "wings"
Of that "whirlybird"
Up above the battles
Listening for that cracklin' word.

"Please come down and help us."
"Get us the hell oughta here!"
And we knew the urgency,
And we felt their fear.

We knew we were the answer
To all of their prayers;
The only way they had out
Was up our "airborne stairs."

So we flew down in the "fire"
Into the brink of hell
To pick up those walking
Who carried those who fell.

They tried not to leave behind
Their buddy and comrade,
But at times couldn't help it
And that was so damned sad.

The ones who shot at them
Were now aiming towards the sky
Trying to shoot us down
As we flew slowly by.

A lot of us made it
And a lot of us died,
But all of us answered the call
And every one of us tried.

We gave support and rescued
Those "grunts" down on the ground,
We saved so many thousands,
But sadly, some were never found.

We were those airborne jockeys
Who flew down through that flack
To try to pick our comrades up
And to try to bring them back.

✦ By Del "Abe" Jones

Del "Abe" Jones served in the United States Air Force, 1958–1961, 92nd Combat Defense Squadron, K-9 Corps, Fairchild Air Force Base, Washington. Although he did not serve during the war in Vietnam, he says he strongly identifies with those who did.

Jones has published three poetry books. He donated the profits from one, *The World, War, Freedom, and More*, to the families of Tennessee National Guardsmen during Desert Storm. This book is still available from Jones via his web site at http://mywebpage.netscape.com/delabejones/page1.html. A second printing of his second book, *Moontides And Other Changes* is scheduled for release.

In addition to having his work featured in newspapers, on radio, and on television, Jones' poems "POW/MIA" and "And, They Were There, Too" is carved in the Ellis County Veteran's Monument in Waxahachie, Texas. See pictures of this monument at http://expage.com/page/delabejones

Today, Jones continues to write poetry and to try to make it in the music business writing song lyrics in White Bluff (Nashville area), Tennessee. His four children and eight grandchildren reside in Spokane, Washington.

📖

Winged Wisdom

ର Always take an overnight bag with you—
you never know where you'll actually end up.
ର Pack a lunch—sometimes you don't make it home.

My Ride to the War

I was in Vietnam constantly being picked up from Landing Zone Betty, or LZ Virginia, or LZ Judy, wherever I had hung my helmet that day, and ferried to war by the Hueys. My platoon or company-sized unit would assemble on the tarmac while a bubble chopper (never knew what they were officially called, never saw one close up; we called them "eye-in-the-sky-choppers") was scouting out battles and the hottest places to insert us. When they found a good place, then would come a long string of Hueys in single file formation, six infantrymen clambering aboard each chopper.

During the flight the noise was usually intense, too much for much talking. Besides, we were always tied up in our own thoughts, in our own worlds, trying to control the butterflies, wondering what the next few minutes would hold, wondering if the LZ would be hot or cold, trying unsuccessfully to not think about the fact that in a few minutes we might well be dead, praying, hoping our families at home wouldn't take it too hard. We seldom knew where we were going, looking out the big open doors as we flew low over farmers and water buffalo out in their rice paddies. Strangely, they seldom looked up, as if a flotilla of Hueys carrying armed-to-the-teeth infantrymen was as commonplace as a swarm of mosquitoes.

When the M-60 machinegun door gunners started firing, we knew we were close, and we started to edge out onto the skids, looking for the place we were to jump. We wanted to get out and away from that helicopter as quickly as we could because those things tended to draw lots of fire. So when the copters swooped in, hovering six feet above the ground, we jumped and ran to form a perimeter of defense in a squatting run, holding our bush caps with one hand and our weapons in the other, till we cleared the rotors' dust-filled backwash.

At the same time, helicopter "killer" gunships with names like "The Jolly Green Giant" blasted away at the tree line. The helicopters that had brought us wasted no time in dee-deeing, hovering but for a moment to disgorge their fighting payload, then they were gone. Too soon it was like they were never there, and we were again alone in the middle of a hostile country. Alone, that is, if we were lucky enough the LZ was a cold one, and we didn't have to dance with the VC (Viet Cong) welcoming committee. If it was a cold LZ, and the battle waited klicks away, again we were left with the eerie feeling of abandonment, with too much time to think of death! I don't know which was the worst, the thinking of fighting and dying or the actual fighting and dying—yeah, I guess I do!

I never knew the crews in the helicopters. They were always rather involved when I saw them from behind their helmets, and it always seemed I never rode with the same crew twice. There was never any conversation between us. They didn't live where the grunts lived. Oh, we were on the same LZ all right, but grunts, when not on patrol, were always on the perimeter in bunkers that were only dirt foxholes with a sandbag roof, while helicopter pilots were somewhere in the middle of the camp in the palace guard buildings, tents, huts or hooches.

Then came the time I thought I'd died. I was humping through a banana plantation on a combat mission when I was severely wounded by a tripwire booby trap, which set off a grenade, that in turn set off an artillery shell—and as I say, ruined my whole day! I was unconscious and close to death, and it was a medevac helicopter we called "Dustoff" that saved my life. It whisked me up and away out of the battle zone posthaste to an aid station where I could receive life-altering care. If it were not for them, if I had to wait very long for some other kind of transportation, maybe a bumpy ride to the OR, I would be surely dead. I was almost dead anyway, but I never saw the helicopter or its crew that saved me. I had an out-of-body experience on the ground, but really only woke up almost three weeks later in Nha Trang. I write of my near-death experience in *I Felt I'd Died*, http://pzzzz.tripod.com/died.html and also printed in *Angels in Vietnam: Women Who Served*.

I had loaded stretchered soldiers, or pieces of soldiers, on the medevacs before, but strangely never thought I'd get to ride in one. It's not healthy to think that, or you'll go crazy. For some odd reason, if you think you're going to get hurt bad, or killed, you never want to go out—funny about that! Then when I did get a ride, I had to sleep through the flight—damn! I did so want to give a fitting goodbye to that country, with a loving farewell gesture—you know, as I watched it disappear from sight out my six!

After Vietnam I have had no experiences with helicopters at all. Even seeing one now brings back too many bad memories. Many men who used to be combat infantrymen tell me even the sight or sound of a helicopter will send them into destructive flashbacks lasting days—days that they are once more back there, once more being delivered to the war by helicopters that are now synonymous with war, once more in the jungle fighting beside their buddies! That makes it hard on marriages, jobs, and relationships!

✝ By Gary Jacobson

Gary Jacobson, "Gazza," is vice president and Awards Committee Coordinator of *The International War Veterans' Poetry Archives* found at http://www.iwvpa.net

Read more of Gary Jacobson's stories and poems in the book *Angels in Vietnam: Women Who Served* and at his web site, *Vietnam Picture Tour* at http://pzzzz.tripod.com/namtour.html

Note: Dee-dee was a very common Vietnamese-French-GI slang meaning to vanish, disappear, get out of here; and dee-dee mau meant to do it very fast, like now. ✝ Gary Jacobson

📖

Eagle Flight

Sitting alone on heated tarmac with brothers
A greenie awaits his first "Eagle Flight,"
Helicopters to carry combat infantrymen
To battles beyond sight…
Waiting,
Listening,
Laughing,
Emptily joking,
Sweating,
Of what's soon to come not speaking,
That whomp whomp whomp sound dreading
Yet ready for the cry rallying,
Waiting for the eagle flight
To carry us to wage the good fight.

We're combat infantrymen bravely ignoring
This herd of elephants down there stomping
Butterflies in the pit of our stomachs
On gossamer wings floating…
In our innards plummet
Romping,
Cavorting.

While we young boys, in full battle gear
Now and then cocking an ear
Are listlessly waiting,
Waiting,
That awful whomp whomp whomp
In nightmarish daydreams hearing
Drumming, drumming, drumming in the fearing.

Knowing somewhere out there in the blue
Eye-in-the-sky choppers flew,
Keeping an eagle's eye looking,
Looking,
Looking for troops in black pajamas.
Looking for action embattled dramas
Searching for Vietcong moving
Searching for Charlies concentrating.
A bevy of huge olive birds
Sent mid dust blown confusion blurred
Would sweep down and pick us up
Giddyup.

Giddyup, and we're off to the war
'Cause war's what we're looking for…
I look out a wide Huey door to try seeing
Where we're going…
Where this sky trooper is being driven
But logistics are given
On a basis of need-to-know,
And grunts just don't need-to-know!

Flying high in the sky...
Emotionless as panoramas pass by
Thinking this war
Sure ain't no bore...
Totally by the awesome sight chilled
In fascination below the clouds skimmed,
Mesmerized at the site hypnotized
Feeling down our necks the heat
In a whomp whomp whomp
Rhythm of jungle beat...

Feeling safe, for the moment...
Each buried in his own thought wondering
What the next moment
Would be bringing
As for the moment of truth readying...
Armaments mentally checking...
Face-to-face, silent prayers saying...
Whomp whomp whomp.

Six brothers ride to war in each Huey.
Not a one thinking now of liberty,
Just hoping to live thru the next few moments,
Adjusting again our armaments,
Hoping to survive
To come out the other end alive
Drawn faces disregarding
Peasants knee deep in rice paddies working,
Ignoring,
Peasants on the road to market to go,
Vietnamese boys riding water buffalo...
Earthbound beings surrounded by green walls
Moving on cut-from-the-jungle halls.

Grim boys psyching for the killing,
No time now for philosophizing,
Watching as horizons closed,
Above earth superimposed.
Far above this microcosm called war.
Strangely "The World" spinning on just as before.

Knowing somewhere out there people are living
Where this sky trooper is being driven,
Of our little bullshit predicament,
Of our life and death involvement,
Of the fear we daily bear,
Totally unaware
Just living their lives without thinking
Wholly without comprehension or care...
Of heartaches America's boys far away bore
In this war-to-end-all war!

Though battle is far,
Quite suddenly here we are.
Suddenly copters are lowering
Brothers climbing on chopper skids readying
To the blow-torched floor to go jumping
Watching rising malignant earth
Praying of Vietcong there's silent dearth,
Hoping the LZ's cold,
Calling up spirits bold,
Bestial hearts pounding,
Adrenaline pumping,
Red blood flowing,
Readying for their very lives running...

Choppers drop us suddenly,
dispassionately,
In the same moment leaving.
Suddenly we're up, we're moving.
Midst din suddenly quieting
Harsh reality replacing dreaming.
The beat of the beast in bodies vibrating
Hearts throbbing
Immediately involved in war's demolition
Lives soon to be lost in bloody attrition
Civilization's abolition
War's unholy perdition...

Nobody tells us where we're going,
Where we'll be toiling.
After all, we're only grunts,
An Army war-dog that hunts.
We're not paid the big bucks for thinking
Just for weapons toting
Good only for dying…
We're battle pawns of callous numbers,
Ground-pounding brothers!

Awaiting us is our goal…
An underground village of Main Force Vietcong
Once annihilated a Vietnamese regiment whole
Who our destiny's to meet all along
Who great carnage dealt in that melee
By these fighting men,
Who once obliterated the French easily,

Men the French called Viet Minh
Just all in all, right friendly folk,
You just had to see…no joke!

When Infantrymen came to visit,
Charlie in his forested pit
Charlie had dee-dee'd
His jungle home abruptly abandoned.
Though brave Infantrymen loudly plead…
Charlie, what gave you your first clue,
We're here looking for you?

Could it have been Cobra gunship's raining fire,
Artillery bringing down your fetid empire,
Jolly Green Giants' mini-guns blazing
Building a hot lead barricade,
Spewing rockets to rain on somebody's parade.
Building a hot lead barricade?
Was it air strikes overhead screaming
The jungle all around you exploding,
Hundreds of troops in your house streaming,

Armed to the teeth assaulting,
Hunting for game,
Just looking for someone to blame.

Charlie, did we make the situation
For you most dire?
Charlie, give us an explanation
Did we your escapade inspire
Spur your ignominious retreat?
Or maybe
You were just going out for a bite to eat.

American infantrymen spent the day humping,
Searching
Hastily abandoned hooches
For weapons, documents, food caches.
Then farewell bade,
Dropped in a grenade,
"Fire in the hole,"
Don't even turn to watch the place blow.

As evening fell,
Eleven platoons took off like bats out of hell.
Leaving one raggedy platoon to man the fort?
Gotta say, didn't give much comfort.
What's up with these day-trippers
Catching commuter choppers,
Taking them away from the war…
Back to where a semblance of sanity will restore,
Transporting them to an LZ's pre-dug foxholes
To piece together what's left of their souls.

This night, 27 brave men would live…or die.
Why did the Army hang us out to fry?
What's that you say,
Impossible is not a term used by the infantry
You say, "Not mine to question why!
Mine just to do or die…"
Bull hockey!

Still, what ya gonna do with the hand you're dealt
We won't be the first, or the last
In this cruel war to go wrong,
To dance to a bitter song.
So dig defensive foxholes in an alien village,
Moments before wreaked and pillaged.
Two thousand surrounding Charlies mad as hell at us
Had to be enraged in a hell of a fuss.
What we did had to make somebody awful mad,
Just a tad…

So, what am I doing here,
Burned in the eyes of 27 desperate men.
What the hell am I doing here
In the home of the Viet Minh.

There's no room for warning trip flares…
No room in the jungle to set claymores.
Are we nothing more than expendable bait?
How soon before we'd know our fate?

Not long I fear…
Not long…
Before Charlies I hear
Tear youthful souls asunder,
Make us pay for seeking plunder
Make us pay for our combat blunder.
Listen to enraged men out there cursing,
Yelling,
Shooting,
Trying to draw our fire,
That they might determine just where we are…
How many of us there are…

They'd likely bust a gut if they only knew
How few
Huddled in the middle of their alien destruction
Once their homes before our unholy conflagration.
They'd laugh and laugh

As like a hot knife through butter they overrun us.
In only a minute bestial legions would kill us,
If they only knew
How few!
But they never knew…
So I'm here to tell the tale,
How I jumped out of the belly of the whale.

The next morning we just humped on out…
Leaving behind frustrated hue and shout.
Moving through elephant grass eye high
Jungle canopies reaching to the sky,
Humping meadows just right for ambushes.
Thick walls of bamboo
Acres of wait-a-minute bushes
Hold you,
Tear at you.

Two Cong up a tree.
Clambered up to see what they could see,
Saw more than they wanted to see.
Surprised just a bit,
By our hasty exit,
Cong snipers fired on our platoon,
Knowing full well suicide
Would visit soon
So we gladly complied
Blowing them away,
Making sure they couldn't fight another day.

Hovering over them face-to-face,
I saw
They had no face.
M-60 machine guns stripped them clean.
These were the first bodies I'd seen.
Only a tatter of clothes remained,
On riddled bodies maimed,
A pink mass of gore…
Nothing more,

Terrible fruits of a terrible war!
And deep in my heart I cried…
Something in me eternally died.
As in the jungle called Le Hong Fong
Life's plans played tragically wrong
In life's most fatal song…

✛ By Gary Jacobson

Note: American soldiers in Vietnam referred to the United States as "the world."

Winged Wisdom

ଔ Just because the sun is shining here, doesn't mean it's shining there.
ଔ If the sun isn't shining here, it might be shining there.
ଔ You can always get there from here.

Answer to a Prayer

In March of 1967, there was a lot of action in Binh Duong Province, in particular, a place known as Ho Bo Woods. This still contained large elements of the politico-military forces of the Viet Cong's Region 4 Headquarters. This area was laced with tunnels and spider holes (camouflaged sniper holes that the VC used). There had been some heavy fighting in this area during the previous 15 months, with no end in sight. Basically, Charlie owned this piece of real estate. He made us pay dearly for every inch of ground we walked on or flew over. This was "Indian Country," and it was not a very good place to be flying alone on any kind of mission. In this area our troops had discovered a large underground complex that included a three-story hospital and offices for the officers, which were all buried under the forest. This was one of those bad places where I could feel the fear creep up my spine, and I could taste it in my mouth anytime I entered the area. It was a very nasty place to do business, and I never looked forward to flying missions into or around it.

On this one particular morning, we had an early start before sunrise. We had been airborne for an hour, but were having a very difficult time locating anything below us in the darkness. When daylight broke over the forest, we had to contend with a thick ground fog that covered everything as far as we could see. Below us looked all white, like a rolling cloud on the ground. We could not see the treetops in most places, so we could not tell if we were flying over an open area or trees. The few LZs (landing zones) inside Ho Bo Woods were small clearings where GIs had cut down the trees or blown them up with explosives, so even the LZs were no bed of roses. They all had tree stumps and fallen logs, which forced us to hover our chopper just a few feet off the ground, so that the troops had to jump out. We also had to throw out the supplies.

We had been flying support for some elements of the 25th Infantry Division on this day. We were all alone, mostly flying single-ship supply missions of fresh food and ammo for the ground troops. We had been concentrating so hard on watching out for Charlie that no one was watching our gas consumption. Needless to say, we had wasted lots of our fuel in a series of long searches, trying to locate the troops.

It was still very early in the morning. The part of the forest we had been flying over was now completely engulfed with heavy, thick fog. There was just no way we could carry on our present mission. We circled around to get our exact bearings and location. The pilots had become a little disoriented by the fog, which covered guiding ground references. The fog was not burning off, but it was slowly rising. It rose upward to around 100 feet or more, just enough so we could not see the treetops anymore. The good news was that no one could see us either, so we were safe from any ground fire.

The bad news was that our fuel warning light had come on with its audio alarm sounding off. The light flashed on the instrument panel as both pilots froze at once. Neither one had any real clue to our present location or where our own troops were below us. We did not have enough fuel to make it out of the fog-shrouded forest. We had no idea which way to turn the aircraft. All directions held a mystery. All the ground below us was hostile and forbidding. There was no right place to go. We were stuck in this twilight zone between certain death and the fog.

We had remaining only about five to 10 minutes of fuel. None of us really knew for sure how much was supposed to be left when the fuel warning light came on. We did not know how much time we had before our aircraft would drop out of the sky into whatever waited for us below. If it were treetops, then our ship would crash and the rotor blades would thrash the trees and twist the body of the helicopter and those inside it. We knew what that would look like because we had seen one of our company ships do that same thing just the week before. That image played over and over inside my head.

The other possibility was that if we could crash land and survive, we would certainly be at a high risk for being captured or killed by enemy troops. It would be a long time before anyone could find and rescue us. The fog would hide our aircraft for hours, and no one would have any idea where we were because we did not even know for sure ourselves.

All these thoughts ran through our minds. Our hearts were pounding like long distance runners in a race we had just lost. I looked around, as I would normally do in this kind of situation, trying to figure out what I might need once we crashed. I grabbed my M-16 rifle and some magazine clips. I wasn't carrying any food or water. We did have lots of colored smoke grenades to use in case we were in need of a rescue attempt. But in this fog, no one would be able to see them.

The pilots had been in radio contact with our other company helicopters, but none of them were close by. That was assuming that our guess about where we were, was in fact, where we actually were. Even after we had given our mayday distress call, no one would be able to quickly respond.

Our fuel should have run out, and we knew we were running on sheer luck. We did not fully understand why we had not dropped out of the sky yet. The fog was endless in all directions. There was just no opening anywhere to be seen. I began to silently talk to God, asking for His divine help to find us someplace to land before we crashed into the forest below.

We were mentally ready for the worse kind of crash. Not knowing what we were falling into gave us no preparation or defense against the certain destruction that came when the rotor blades tore the aircraft apart.

Out of nowhere, just below us where we had already looked, there was a clear opening over a grassy meadow area—a perfect LZ to drop down into. We turned and lined up with the LZ just as the engine died, having consumed its last ounce of jet fuel. The helicopter was less than 25 feet from the ground, and the blades were still rotating with enough force that we did not drop very hard. There was no damage—a perfect landing, in fact.

I immediately jumped out of the ship as it hit, taking my weapon with me. Around the tree-lined meadow we saw movement everywhere. Our helicopter was completely surrounded. We were on the ground, ready to defend ourselves, but there was no way we were going to win this battle. We were completely outnumbered and surrounded. Any resistance on our part would have been a death warrant for sure, so we just held our position and waited.

Then we began to notice the uniforms they were wearing. They were elements of the 25th Infantry. By some unbelievable luck, we had dropped right on top of one of their small temporary camps. We couldn't have been more blessed if we had tried. Not only were we surrounded by our own troops, but they also had a supply of JP-4 jet fuel for our helicopter.

It was a strange experience and hard to explain. For example, why did this LZ just open up in the middle of so many square miles of solid fog? Why was there a clearing at this spot waiting for us? Why hadn't our helicopter run out of fuel before we saw this opening? Why had we not seen this opening before when we were looking in that same area?

It was a very lucky or blessed day, depending on how you viewed the events. Just good luck you might say, maybe? But then, perhaps other forces were at work. Maybe the power of a small silent prayer opened a big hole in the fog? I do not know for sure why it all happened as it did. I do know that we did not crash, and no one was killed or injured—and that was good enough for me. I do not need anyone to tell me that prayers do work—I believe.

✦ By Bill McDonald
  The Vietnam Experience, http://www.vietnamexp.com
  LZ Angel, http://www.lzangel.com

"Answer to a Prayer" is reprinted here, with permission, from Bill McDonald's book, *A Spiritual Warrior's Journey*. See Bill McDonald's stories in this book, "The First Unofficial Bombing Raid of Cambodia" and "All Washed Up in Georgia," chapter 1; and "Life or Death Decision," chapter 7.

Winged Wisdom

ର Get a pet—someone who loves you whether or not you fly.

Cosmic Code

For almost 300 combat hours
I perched in gilded Huey cages
sometimes in God's empty seat
sometimes just 50mm from the gunner
hovering above the skid rows below.

Those long and loud isolation tank flights
gave rare privy to my own thoughts
as I stared at the dots and dashes
of hectares and graves
that were surely some cosmic code
that,
once cracked,
would yield secrets
only I would know.

✦ By Pat Hewatt

"I used to fly and hang out the side from the gunner's seat and look down and really think I was going to see something that would tell me an answer to the many unanswerable questions I had." ✦ Pat Hewatt

Pat Hewatt went to Vietnam, 1967–1968, as a Donut Dolly, recreational specialist in the Supplemental Recreational Activities Overseas Division of the American Red Cross. Pat Hewatt is the author of *Seasons of Siege,* a book of poetry. Her writings also are published in *Angels in Vietnam: Women Who Served.* Read more of Pat Hewatt's poetry at *American Red Cross Vietnam Donut Dollies,* http://www.donutdolly.com. Since Vietnam, she has worked as a copywriter and editor, and she is now Director of Communications at a state psychiatric hospital. She lives with her German Shepherd, Riley.

📖

Whirling Blades

Every war, it appears, has its own characteristic trigger—some small event, usually associated with hearing or smell, that ignites in its veterans a set of emotions and memories, a kind of flashback.

After WWI, the smell of decay brought back the trench war to its survivors. For Normandy veterans, the smell of apples (from the French orchards?) always brought back D-Day. For me, the smell of every gas station with a diesel pump plays a mental Viet Nam tape in my head; but the sound of whirling helicopter blades is the worst.

In Nam, I could ID them from klicks away, the Hueys, the LOHs (Light Observation Helicopters), the Cobras, the Chinooks. Back here, after 25 years,

I've grown older, the chopper has evolved, and I can't tell 'em apart anymore. But I can still hear 'em before I can see 'em and there's always that "Oh, Jesus!" feeling in the pit of my stomach.

Standing in a crowd, you can tell who's "been there" by watching their eyes when a chopper flies over.

✠ By James M. Hopkins

Hopkins served with the 1st Infantry Division and 9th Infantry Division, RVN (Republic of Vietnam, South Vietnam), 1969–1970. Today, he is happily married to Deanna Gail Shlee Hopkins. Between them, they have five children and eleven grandchildren.

Read Hopkins' "For All Our Brothers Who Fell From the Sky," chapter 6.

James M. Hopkins' poetry, and his wife's story, "Deanna's Love Story," are published in *Angels in Vietnam: Women Who Served.*

See more of Hopkins' and his wife's stories and poetry at *A Circle of Friends* at http://gecko.gc.maricopa.edu/~dgshleeh

"*Circle* was created to publish writings by our 'circle of friends' about any subject, not just Vietnam War related." ✠ James M. Hopkins

To read Hopkins' poetry, visit *The Sound of Whirling Blades—Poems and Reflections* at

http://vets.appliedphysics.swri.edu/blades.htm

http://www.vietvet.org/blades.htm (mirror site)

part of *The Vietnam Veterans Home Page* at http://vets.appliedphysics.swri.edu

CHAPTER 3

Australian Memories

There are no signposts in the sky
to show a man has passed that way before.
There are no channels marked.
The flier breaks each second into new uncharted seas.

Anne Morrow Lindbergh, 1906-2001
North to the Orient

Private Fisher: M.I.A.

(Prologue:
He looked at me with vacant eyes
in my dreams the other night
and I felt again the deepest pain
since he disappeared from sight.)

The Incident:
More than thirty years ago,
in September sixty-nine,
Private Fisher fell into the hell
that veiled him for all time.

We'd got a call to support a slick
that had to extract a patrol of five.
In rappelling ropes rested hopes
that they'd make it out alive.

The chopper hovered overhead;
the rappelling ropes were lowered.
Out ran the five, they would survive,
they'd soon be home and showered.

They appeared above the canopy,
dangling eighty feet beneath the skids.
A sigh of relief became a cry of grief;
from the rope Private Fisher slid.

I did not hear his screams or yells,
I could not see his frightened face.
I saw him fall, bounce like a ball…
swallowed by jungle without a trace.

The Army inserted two companies;
for a week they searched in vain.
Nothing was found, neither sight nor sound.
He was never seen again.

Epilogue:
I never met the soldier
who fell from the ropes that day;
But in my mind and for all time
that scene will e'er replay.

His vacant eyes still haunt me
and the pain scores deep, my soul.
After each dream I quietly scream;
and my mind and blood run cold.

Postscript:
Near the Memorial on the Avenue of Honour
are six plaques set in concrete blocks.
In words sublime, they record for all time
six Aussies who never came back.

Michael Herbert
Robert Carver
Richard Parker
Peter Gilson
David Fisher
John Gillespie

✦ By Anthony W. Pahl, written 14 July 2002

📖

Winged Wisdom

☞ Others may call you courageous; however, you know
that you sometimes have no other options but to be brave.

Red and Green Christmas

Christmas Day, 1969, started early for Albatross 07. The slick had red and white stripes painted on it, the Red Cross parcels and Santa had been loaded at Kanga Pad, and it was 0530. We had a long morning and a lot of sorties ahead of us. I was eagerly looking forward to the little joy we could present to the diggers in the field.

Our first stop was Fire Support Base (FSB) Digger's Rest, east of the province. The red dust swirled as the pilot pulled back on the collective to flare out. We didn't want to stay too long, there was a contact the night before, but we had a special mission and that was important. All the blokes who weren't on either sentry duty or patrol gathered around the chopper, and the smiles on their faces as Santa handed out the gifts was a joy to behold.

Next was FSB Coral. Again a feeling of worthiness settled on the chopper crew as we took off, heading for a lager of APCs (armored personnel carrier) and ground-pounders who had been on patrol for five days looking for a guy who fell off the rappelling ropes during a hot extraction a few days earlier. What a gift for all if they found him—but they never did. I've lived with his memory at Christmas for a long time because he was hanging on my ropes on my chopper when he fell.

We landed in a clearing that the Cavalry had made for us, and Santa began to hand out gift parcels and Christmas cheer with the accompanying "Ho! Ho! Ho!"

As he and his flying-suited elf helpers were handing over extra ones for those who were just departing on patrol, the chopper was rocked by an enormous shock wave.

Blokes dived for cover, most clutching the parcels as if they were the last contact that they would ever have from home.

I looked around. An APC was on its side and on fire. Mind-chilling screams were coming from it. Agony, fear, horror—screams like nothing on earth—thirty yards from where I was.

"Get in, we're out o' here."

"No way!"

"That's an order!"

"Go without me."

The APC hit a land mine. No incoming, just fear.

I raced to the APC. Checked the driver. He seemed unconscious. I dragged him out. It was easy. The bottom half of him, well it wasn't there. He blinked once. Then nothing. I ran to the turret. A bloke with a helmet was crawling out. I helped him. "Inside," he said.

I raced to the back. Peered in where the ramp had buckled. Blood. Hands over faces. Blood from eyes, ears, mouths. More blokes arrived to help. It was hot. I had a Nomex fireproof flying suit and gloves. I smoked. We forced the ramp open. I went inside and helped the guys to get out.

Then it was over. One was dead—the driver. Some with ruptured eardrums and other compression injuries and burns. Amazingly, there were no broken bones or shrapnel wounds.

I was in trouble. Knew it. I disobeyed. But the chopper was still there. We called for "Dustoff," replaced all the parcels with wounded and took off for Nui Dat. Two more Dustoffs required.

Nothing was ever said about my actions. I was relieved to be let off the hook.

But every year at this time—it happens again.

Not shared this before. Can now.

✝ By Anthony W. Pahl, written 27 December 1999

True Blue

This story's of two youths,
both in their late teens,
who went to war in Vietnam
and saw amazing scenes.
Both youths were nicknamed Blue
because of their red hair.
This story relates an experience
that both of them once shared.

One Blue was in the Army, the other in the RAAF.
Both volunteered for service
because they were young and brash.

The Army Blue was infantry and trained in ground warfare.
He learned to use a rifle and at tracking had a flair.
As lead scout he became the best and always led with care.
He scoured the jungle twilight with eyes always aware.

On one patrol he felt that things were not exactly right.
A churning feeling in his gut told him they'd have to fight.
So he led with greater care but nothing could he see
'til suddenly the jungle lit just like a Christmas tree.

He felt a burning pain all down his left hand side.
He fell down on the jungle track with no place he could hide.
He heard the shout of "Contact!"
He heard the yells of mates.
He wondered at the agony.
He wondered at his fate.

Now when the other Blue arrived in Vietnam
he decided that the jungle was no fit place for man.
He applied for chopper duties so he could fly above.
As a chopper gunner he excelled a job he came to love.

Then one day they got a call—a "Dust-off" was required.
A patrol had sprung an ambush and was pinned down under fire.
By the time the chopper got there the fight had died right down.
But the chopper had to hover above the jungle crown.

"Throw smoke."
"Smoke thrown!"
"Blue smoke?"
"Correct!"

So the litter was winched down
on a hundred feet of cable through the jungle to the ground.

Blue held onto the winch control—his heart tight in his chest.
The cable jerked—the signal sent to raise the litter fast.
But bullets were buzzing all around and thumped into the skin.
The litter was only half way up. Was there time to winch it in?

Blue's finger touched the button to cut the winching wire.
Lose one man hanging down below or risk a funeral pyre?

"Ascend! Ascend! Straight up! Don't think!" Blue yelled into the mike.
"We'll have to risk him through the trees. Break! Break from the fight!"

The chopper rose—but tilted right—the litter caught a snag.
"Move left! Move left! We'll free him yet. Not another body bag!"

The chopper jerked—the litter freed.
Blue winched him all the way.
"He's in! He's safe—let's move it to the hospital on the bay."

Blue took a breath deep in his chest
and sighed with huge relief.
He turned his eyes to look upon the bloke who'd come to grief.

Tears fell down from both their cheeks as they stared at one another. "Made it!" he sighed as they both cried.

Blue had saved his younger brother.

✦ By Anthony W. Pahl, written 27 July 1993

I dedicate this poem to Alan Maxwell Pahl, my younger brother by 10½ months—we were both born in 1950.

This poem is not factual; it is an allegory of the horrors that the Vietnam War inflicted and still inflicts on all warriors and families of warriors.

Alan and I were both Royal Australian Air Force airmen trained as Airfield Defence Guards. We served together in Vung Tau, SVN, at the same time though Alan arrived in country about 6 months after me and I became a helicopter gunner, whereas Alan elected to remain in his primary job as that of an Air Force soldier.

I wrote this poem during one of my extended hospitalization periods when I was really missing him. Until Vietnam, we were as close as two brothers could possibly be; I joined the RAAF (Royal Australian Air Force) in December 1967, he joined in February 1968. I enlisted as an Airfield Defence Guard, so did he. I completed my ADG training and was posted to the RAAF Base at Richmond, NSW—so was he. I was then posted to Vietnam, so was he. I came home, so did he.

But we had changed and I have only seen him about four times since Vietnam—31 years ago; the most recent occasion was at our father's funeral 10 years ago, where we barely said g'day. I truly miss him.

✦ Anthony W. Pahl

Anthony W. Pahl, an Australian Vietnam veteran, served with the Royal Australian Air Force, No. 9 Squadron, Vung Tau/Nui Dat, 1969–1970, as a helicopter gunner and leading aircraftsman.

For more stories, poems, and pictures from Anthony W. Pahl, visit his web site, *Bushranger's Revetment*, at http://www.the-revetment.net. More of Pahl's poetry also is included in the *International War Veterans' Poetry Archives*, http://www.iwvpa.net. Anthony Pahl, "Bushranger," is the senior vice president and webmaster of the *IWVPA*.

Pahl's poetry also is published in *Angels in Vietnam: Women Who Served*.

📖

Flight Facts: The United States wasn't the only country to send their sons and daughters to the aid of South Vietnam. In the early 1960s, Australia and New Zealand also sent troops to the war.

More than 50,000 Australian military personnel, including 200 female nurses, served in Vietnam from 1962–1973. An estimated 3,000 Australians were wounded during this time and approximately 500 lost their lives in country.

From 1966–1971, Australia sent 192 (rotating 48 men per year) Navy helicopter pilots and crew members to Vietnam to serve with America's 135th Assault Helicopter Company out of Fort Hood, Texas. During the war, Australia also had helicopter crews serving with the Royal Australian Air Force, No. 9 Squadron.

The New Zealand government did not keep records of the Royal New Zealand Air Force personnel who served in Vietnam. Historians estimate that approximately 4,500 New Zealanders served in Vietnam. Of these, 39 did not make it home alive.

CHAPTER 4

Heroes

*Our nation is indeed fortunate
that we can still draw on an immense reservoir
of courage, character, and fortitude.*

Ronald Reagan, 1911–present

Winged Wisdom

⇣ If you are a pilot, teach your crew chief to fly and navigate.
⇣ If you are a crew chief, teach your pilot about engines and navigating.

The Unsung Heroes of the Flight Line

When most people think about helicopters and what they do, they usually think of some hotshot pilot doing all kinds of tricky maneuvers. What many fail to consider is that the pilot wouldn't even be getting off the ground were it not for the crew chief and door gunner making it happen.

They are the ones who are at the flight line hours before takeoff time, checking out and fine-tuning the aircraft to make sure everything is operational. They are the ones who stay at the flight line for hours, sometimes late into the night, cleaning the aircraft and armament systems so it'll be ready for the next day's mission.

They are the ones who are stuck in the cargo bay of the aircraft at the mercy of whomever their pilot may be, as well as being wide open to enemy fire. Uncle Sam thought about providing armored seats and sliding chicken plates for the pilots, but must have dozed off when it came time to provide a similar type of protection for the crew.

It was a long time before this dawned on me. I took too much for granted. For that error in judgment I would like to apologize to all the crews who did the hard part, usually with little recognition or appreciation. They are the people who made the whole thing come together. They, on many occasions, were the ones with the brains and intestinal fortitude to make things happen in order to have a successful mission. I salute you all and cannot heap enough praise on you for the brave and magnificent job you did in Vietnam.

You were truly *The Unsung Heroes of the Flight Line!*

✦ By Tom Nesbitt
   Pilot, 335th AHC "Cowboys," RVN 1970–1971
   http://www.angelfire.com/ga/cowboy16/index.html

Read Tom Nesbitt's poem "Lone Slick" and his story "There I Was in Vietnam," chapter 5.

📖

Everyone's a Hero

I have no tales of heroics, because I flew in a place where every young man and woman was a hero. I have only the memories of patriotic young people who were willing to risk it all for a country that turned its back on them.

✦ Bob Mackey, Dustoff pilot, RVN 1969–1970
   Read Bob Mackey's story, "God's Fingerprint," chapter 9.

📖

Winged Wisdom

☙ Don't try to be a hero—if you are one, you can't plan it.
☙ Have a mentor; be a mentor.
☙ Make a positive difference in someone else's life.

The True Nature of Courage

Teaching at a continuation high school for the last five years has given me an extraordinary insight into the state of our current society. While I was studying for my teaching credential, one instructor commented to the class that we shouldn't blame the kids for what they didn't know.

"They don't know the rules," the instructor would thunder in class after class as he brought home the point that it was our responsibility to teach them "The Game." Even though I believe that he was right in principle, I have sadly concluded that most of the adult world in this country knows even less than the kids about many things, primarily the true nature of courage.

This country is obsessed with a celebrity subculture. Somehow excessive adoration of the popular and famous has mutated into the belief that the simple act of making money by throwing a ball, portraying some real or imagined person on the silver screen and television, or by stretching the bounds of civility to the breaking point is "Heroic." Movie stars become "American Heroes" or worse yet, "Legends," and talented athletes are heralded as "Sports Heroes." Most dictionaries actually use words like "bold action" to define a hero, and I agree. However, the definitions all leave out what I regard as another important component of real heroics—that the act of heroism must have been performed with knowledge of the risk to one's physical well-being. Celebrity figures are pampered entertainers. Everything is calculated with an eye to the bottom line (fame and money). Real heroes do not play to an audience. They do what they must because it is what is expected of them. In order to teach our children "the rules," I want to tell them what I think constitutes a real hero.

This is a war story, but not your usual war story. There are no blazing guns or exploding bombs falling all around. No enemy troops are rushing the American lines. My story is about a routine helicopter flight on a freight-hauling mission during the Vietnam War. This flight thrust the crew into the jaws of Hell. The lives of everyone aboard were at stake on that fateful day of March 12, 1967, ten thousand miles from Hollywood.

This is the story of a U.S. Army CH-47 Chinook helicopter, 62-2132, that was lifting a 105mm artillery piece on an external sling with the eight members of the gun crew riding along inside the aircraft. There were five additional crew members: two pilots, a flight engineer, a crew chief, and a gunner. Shortly after loading the gun crew and sling loading the artillery piece, a hand grenade carried by one of the artillery crewmen fell to the floor about 10 minutes into the flight. No big deal except that he had pulled the safety pin and put a rubber band around the grenade to hold the handle in place. The rubber band broke when the grenade hit the floor and it exploded in the airborne CH-47. All of the artillery people along with one of the aircraft crew members who were riding in the cargo bay were severely wounded. The left gunner was not wounded because he was shielded by one of the artillery gun crew. Newt Coryell, the flight engineer, was not hit since he was lying on the floor looking out an open hatch at the artillery piece on the sling. Pilots John Caron and Harold Miller were not wounded since they were up front and were shielded from the blast. After the explosion the Chinook made a forced return to the landing zone they had just left.

This is where the story takes on heroic proportions, and even though I was a CH-47 flight engineer for most of my time in Vietnam, I had never faced anything quite like this. I can't honestly say that I would have done the same thing that this crew did in this circumstance. At first glance the crew seemed to do the logical thing given the situation. They decided not to wait on medevac choppers to take away the wounded. Instead, they performed a quick check of the big Chinook (without shutting down) to determine if she was still airworthy; then the wounded were flown to the nearest hospital, thereby saving precious time for the injured soldiers. Because of potential damage from the explosion it would have been very easy for Newt to simply say that he could not guarantee the airworthiness of the Chinook. Warrant Officer Miller wanted to take the wounded back to Vung Tau, and Major Caron supported the decision. Newt was not in disagreement, but had he insisted that the aircraft was not airworthy it "may" have lead to a re-evaluation of the decision to go to Vung Tau. Whether any wounded soldiers would have been adversely affected by a decision to call the medevac helicopters will remain pure speculation since they did fly the wounded back to Vung Tau.

This is a story about courage because not Newt, not John Caron, nor Harold Miller took the easy way out. This desperate situation did not allow time for a thorough examination of the aircraft. Since Newt made this quick inspection with the aircraft running, it was impossible to be thorough. The check was very incomplete since none of the cowling was opened. There simply was no time. I, too, was a flight engineer, and although this may have seemed like a very logical thing to do, it was not. I know what Newt knew. There were several holes visible in the aircraft. It was easy to assume that a U.S. Army fragmentation grenade had done some considerable damage, even if it was not readily apparent. The question of whether a fuel line had been punctured or nicked near the engine could not be answered with any degree of certainty at the moment. There are three hydraulic systems on a CH-47. Two of them are for the flight controls and the third one is a utility system. Newt was looking at a couple of hundred yards of hydraulic lines that could be damaged even though the hydraulic gauges in the cockpit indicated that all three systems were maintaining pressure. The major question for Newt was whether they would all hold long enough to complete this flight. Loss of the utility system would mean that they would land with no brakes. An awkward situation, but something that could be managed. The loss of one flight control system was something to be concerned about but did not mean death. Loss of the second flight control system while in flight was guaranteed fatal. The loss of hydraulic pressure was not the only concern with those systems. The failure of a hydraulic fitting or a line in a particular area could result in a fine, high-pressure spray, which could cause a catastrophic fire similar to what a fuel leak can do. While all of this would not necessarily be deadly, Newt and the pilots had enough problems that day. Miles of electrical wire that may also have been damaged were of great concern, and Newt had no time to consider whether one or two electrical systems or even the whole electrical complex would collapse and set the aircraft on fire.

Now we come to something that every CH-47 flight engineer, at some time during his career, fears may happen to him one day. A Chinook is a very complicated aircraft. The drive shaft system, which connects the engines to the rotor heads, uses an elaborate system of five transmissions and nine pieces of drive shafting. The flight engineer's nightmare is the five sections that connect the combining box transmission at the forward base of the aft pylon across the top of the helicopter up to the forward transmission. These shafts spin at more than 7,000 revolutions per minute with less then an inch clearance between the shaft and floor of the tunnel area they pass through. In fact, most crew members I have known could not slip their pinky finger comfortably between the drive shaft tunnel floor and the bottom of the shaft. If anything metallic came between the floor of that shaft tunnel and one of the spinning aluminum shafts it would only take seconds to destroy the shaft and cause the blades to lose their synchronization. Using Chinook talk this is called "dephasing." To an observer it appears that the Chinook explodes in flight when this happens. Thankfully, this situation is extremely rare.

I tell this story today because the actions of these brave men bespeak the real nature of heroism. To take immediate and unselfish action in the face of impending danger is the true nature of courage. Police and fire personnel know very well what I'm talking about. They do it everyday, and it is regarded as routine and part of the job by many in American society. Unfortunately, our kids are not learning the difference between a "sports role model" and a "real hero." Real heroes are not considered "cool." I know Newt Coryell and John Caron. Unfortunately, I never knew the late Harold Miller. Most students in my classroom would not consider any of these men to be "cool." I can personally attest to the fact that they weren't "cool" 34 years ago either. I can't imagine either Newt or John as the life of the party. They, like many of the Americans in Vietnam, were professionals with high standards. They could be counted on to put everything on the line and to do what was required when disaster struck. They didn't brag, they didn't look for the spotlight, and they didn't crave attention. They simply knew their jobs and they did them well.

I want my students to see this story. Hopefully some of them will read it and begin to question themselves about some of their "heroes." Others, with little or no understanding, will simply laugh it off as a military fantasy. I am now 54 years old and have learned that what popular culture thinks doesn't really matter. Eternal truths remain eternal whether popular culture accepts them or not. What the crew of 62-2132 did that day in March of 1967 once again validated the true nature of courage. I will continue to fight popular culture and its myths so that my students will learn the difference between "role models" and "heroes."

As for Newt and John, they may not have Shaq O'Neal's money or fame, but they have something much more precious. They have the knowledge of themselves and the respect of people who don't count human worth by the size of people's bank accounts or their exposure in the media. Shaq may in fact show himself one day to be a real hero. I, however, prefer to stick with the proven product. Thank you, gentlemen, for allowing me to serve with you.

✢ By Rodney R. Brown
   147th ASHC Hillclimber Veterans' Association, http://www.147thhillclimbers.org

📖

Flight Facts: The CH-47 Chinook tandem-rotor cargo helicopter was designed by Boeing in 1956. It was first used by the military in Vietnam in 1962 and is still in use today for large payload internal-and external-capability transportation of weapons, equipment, and troops.

CHAPTER 5

Slicks

*We soon saw that the helicopter had no future, and dropped it…
The helicopter is much easier to design than the aeroplane,
but is worthless when done.*

Wilbur Wright, 1867–1912

Flight Facts: The first test flight of Bell Helicopter Textron's XH-40 utility model helicopter was October 22, 1956. This was the birth of the UH-1 Iroquois "Huey." Less than a decade later, it was the most widely used helicopter in the military. From the time the Hueys began arriving in Vietnam in 1963 until the end of the war, more than 7,000 of these versatile helicopters flew more than seven and a half million hours. They were used for medevac, troop transport, command and control, air assault, and even as gunships. The Huey continues to serve the military as an airworthy and versatile helicopter. Bell produced more than 10,000 Huey aircraft, many of which are still flown today in more than three dozen countries.

Lone Slick

At first a dark speck in the clear blue sky,
The Huey descends from its safety on high.
The pilot now spots his small LZ ahead,
A hole in the jungle evokes feelings of dread.

A one-ship insertion with no gunships along
Is never safe, lots of things could go wrong.
He drops to low level a mile from the spot,
Skimming the treetops, he's done this a lot.

The lower and faster he flies near the ground,
Increases the odds he will take fewer rounds.
A scan of the instruments says all there is well,
On short final approach to a hover in hell.

A quick glance around and the LZ looks cold,
But one never knows in a tight hover hole.
Instinct tells him that it's time for his flare,
A last look around cause there's no room for error.

The slick rears up, like a part of his body,
Stands on its tail, it's no time to be shoddy.
The hole in the jungle will hold only one ship,
As the nose slowly falls into place with a dip.

The rotor blades chop off a palm tree branch,
Insuring an exit without taking more chance.
The gunners are scanning the tree lines around,
Be sure that ole Charlie was not to be found.

The intercom squawks with a "Clear right and left, Sir,"
A sigh of relief from the crew as the winds stir.
The slick settles in to a high six-foot hover,
The saw grass so thick is blown back to uncover.

The brilliant white flash 'neath the pilot's chin bubble,
Plexiglas flying, they all know they're in trouble.
White hot shrapnel cuts deep in his legs,
As four grunts jump off and four more renege.

A booby trap bomb had just ruined a nice day,
Beneath the saw grass it was hidden away.
His training had taught him to be wary of this,
One hole in the jungle held death's deadly kiss.

Sudden reflex results in a pulling of power,
To a thirty-foot hover as things start going sour.
This giving the pilot a quick look around,
Back down he goes to put more grunts aground.

But two have been hit, leaving two to insert,
Get out of here now and check on the hurt.
The instrument panel is flashing its lights,
Saying, "Out of here now, come back later to fight."

The wide Mekong River is directly behind,
A quick pedal turn with an engine that whines.
He follows the river back toward safety and home,
The slick's making noises in its guts like a groan.

Warning lights, buzzers will drive you insane,
Getting bent out of shape will mess up your brain.
The airfield's in sight now but low RPM,
At one hundred knots he low levels on in.

A long running landing seems logical now,
As the skids slide along, the engine goes POW!
He slides fifty yards and slowly drags to a stop,
Then dreams of cold beer, fifteen cents a pop.

✦ By Tom Nesbitt
   Pilot, 335th AHC "Cowboys," RVN 1970–1971
   http://www.angelfire.com/ga/cowboy16/index.html

📖

Winged Wisdom

∝ You can fly anywhere.
∝ Attention to details can save your life.

There I Was in Vietnam

I joined the Georgia National Guard in 1960. In early 1968, the Army sent a letter to local Guard units asking for volunteers. It seems some place in Southeast Asia I had never heard of was putting Uncle Sam in a bind. Feeling young, 27, and infallible, I called the Pentagon and offered myself up for sacrifice, providing I could attend helicopter training. It worked.

During the third week of Ranger School (which due to some genetic defect I volunteered for) I was injured in a training accident. Two weeks later I began the Infantry Officers Basic Course; after this I attended Airborne School, becoming the "Outstanding Student Graduate" (a little statue and a "good" letter in my files).

Finally, Flight School at Fort Wolters, Texas, and Hunter Army Airfield at Savannah, Georgia, and then Vietnam. Reality was not the six o'clock news or John Wayne movies. I should mention, when I left for Vietnam, I left behind my wife and three small children, ages 7, 6, and 2.

Upon arriving in Vietnam, I was immediately assigned to the 335th Assault Helicopter Company (Cowboys) at Bearcat, about 25 miles from Long Binh. I served there as executive officer until late August when the unit moved to Dong Tam in the central Delta.

After arriving at Dong Tam, a new captain came in with date of rank on me, therefore taking over the XO (executive officer) position. This put me as 1st platoon leader (Ramrods), and I was able to get in much more flying time, which is what everybody wanted anyway. Nightly mortar and 122mm rocket attacks were the norm at Dong Tam, which was considerably more remote and less secure than Bearcat had been. The U.S. 9th Infantry Division had recently left Dong Tam and rotated back to the States as part of the gradual withdrawal plan for U.S. infantry units. The 7th ARVN (Army of the Republic of Vietnam) Division was now responsible for base security. I'm sure this made Charlie very happy.

In mid-December, I transferred to the 114th Assault Helicopter Company (Knights) at Vinh Long, farther up the Mekong River. Here, I was assigned to the Red Knights, flying slicks on combat assaults in the same general area of operations as before. In mid-February I was offered the job of assistant airfield commander at Vinh Long Airfield. This is not as important a job as it sounds, but was a short-timer's dream. The most hazardous duty I did here was to police up dud mortar rounds from the airstrip in the mornings and haul them by jeep off the airfield to the EOD (Explosive Ordnance Disposal) for disposal. The mortar rounds were so rusty that many failed to detonate on impact. After all, they had probably been hand carried from Hanoi all the way down the Ho Chi Minh Trail to the southernmost part of Vietnam. I still got in some good flying time though.

The calendar countdown began, and I found myself on the way back to the real world on 15 May 1970. After about a year with the 82nd Airborne Division at Fort Bragg, North Carolina, I was honorably discharged from service and returned with my family to my hometown of Cordele in southern Georgia.

Here, I was employed by the U.S. Postal Service until my retirement in August of 1986. I still reside in Cordele, Georgia.

In retrospect, my volunteering for Vietnam seemed to be a really dumb thing to do. However, if I had it to do all over again, I'd still do it. I have no regrets.

✦ By Tom Nesbitt
  Pilot, 335th AHC "Cowboys," RVN 1970–1971
  http://www.angelfire.com/ga/cowboy16/index.html

Read Tom Nesbitt's tribute to "The Unsung Heroes of the Flight Line," chapter 4.

📖

Flight Facts: An estimated 40,000 helicopter pilots served in the Vietnam War. Nearly 5,000 helicopter pilots, crew chiefs, and door gunners lost their lives in combat and operational accidents in what was known as the first helicopter war.

Winged Wisdom

ଓ Always let someone else know where you're
headed, in case you don't arrive there.
ଓ Be nice to your crew chief.
ଓ Be nice to your pilot.

Trick or Treat

It was a warm, humid Halloween morning, October 31, 1970. I had some eggs and java at the mess tent while talking to my door gunner; we were about to start another day of flying. Dick was not my regular gunner, but I knew he could shoot and keep it together under fire—a most important asset. I also knew he had just come off his second helicopter crash. I really didn't give that much thought, not having been through one myself. Hell, if Dick was still flying after that, he must have nerves of steel.

Dick and I made small talk about getting back to the "world" (home) and maybe shooting some bad guys if the opportunity presented itself. Flying ash and trash missions this day was safer than any combat assault or insertion-type sortie. That was fine with us, this would be an easy day, and when we returned this evening we would have one hell of a Halloween Party to go to in the hangar.

There were going to be all the steaks and booze we could consume and a band complete with strippers. In Vietnam, we had to grab the fun when we could. This would be a great evening with a good alcohol-induced sleep.

We left the mess tent and went back to the hooch to retrieve our M-16s, side arms, and two heavy M-60 machine guns. It was amazing how heavy those machine guns were. We had to walk a half mile to my helicopter, so we had a good sweat by the time we arrived. The fire retardant uniform (Nomex) we wore dried quickly and gave us time to escape a helicopter fire, which unfortunately is all too common in post-crash accidents. With the helmet on, collar up, and visor down, the only exposed skin is the chin and nose.

We arrived at my helicopter at 0600 hours, and I helped Dick mount the two machine guns. I had already loaded 3,000 rounds per gun the night before, so all we had to do was lock and load as soon as we cleared our airfield. I continued opening up my helicopter, removed the inlet covers, and took the fuel sample. Dick's responsibility ended with the guns. He was a gunner, not a Huey crew chief. Because of that, he knew if we came under fire, we would keep the enemy on his side of the aircraft while engaging. The copilot also rode the right side, and this is because out of the four of us, the copilot (aka Peter Pilot, "PP") and the gunner were easier to replace than the aircraft commander or crew chief. Sounds a little cold, but most gunners I knew would have it no other way. As far as the copilot's feelings go, well, that is the price he paid for being a new guy. Anyway, the sooner he learned the flying business, the sooner he would get a left seat for himself.

The pilots arrived—a 21-year-old aircraft commander called Bullet (because he was playing around with his grease gun in his hooch and accidentally fired a complete clip of .45 caliber through his roof) and a new guy, Mr. Tibbs, who was basically there for the ride. He had not yet earned a nickname and was still a cherry due to the good fortune of not having been under fire yet. Mr. Tibbs had only been there a month; he would get his chance.

Bullet and I, on the other hand, had a great relationship—when things got hot we did not need to talk to one another. We had been under fire before, and we had the same desire to go home at the end of our tour riding in the passenger area of the plane, not the baggage hold. Bullet was from Idaho and I am from Washington, so we were almost homeboys. He called me Teddy Bear because I looked so young. That was okay with me as long as we were flying. I did, however, prefer to be called Chief, for that is what all pilots call their crew chief. We were as close-knit a team as one will ever find. Our lives depended on each of us doing our jobs, especially when under fire or in case of mechanical trouble. The pilots put their lives in my hands, so I had to keep the Huey in top shape. I counted on them to get us home safely each day without hitting a mountain or wires, and to get us on the ground safely should we fall from the sky. We all counted on the gunner to shoot straight without jamming and to keep both guns functioning as they were designed.

The pilots completed their preflight inspection, including both machine guns. I always wondered if they actually knew what the hell they were looking for when they looked at an M-60 machine gun. Oh well. It was a moot point because the guns had already passed my inspection, or I would have relieved my gunner—something I never had to do.

We got strapped in and it was time to rock and roll. Mr. Tibbs pulled the starting trigger and Satellite 318 started to come to life. After a couple of minutes of running and a quick crosscheck of all instruments, we were ready to cheat death one more day and fly the friendly skies of Southeast Asia.

Mr. Tibbs got the order from Bullet to call the tower for departure: "Long Thanh tower, Satellite 318 for a south departure."

We took off to the south. As soon as we cleared the safety of our compound, Dick and I locked and loaded our guns and pulled them down at the ready. We climbed to 1,500 feet as quickly as possible to get us out of .30 caliber range. Most helicopters were shot down by small arms and below 1,500 feet. At the same time, Bullet gave the command to test-fire the guns. This was a normal daily routine which I enjoyed because I wanted my gunner to have something to do that night, such as cleaning his guns. Hell, I would be up until 2300 getting my aircraft ready for the next day. I grabbed both triggers and brought her to life. I let about 100 rounds go and watched as the tracers danced to the rice paddy below. I heard Dick's guns do the same, and even though it was a test, we could feel the adrenaline starting to pump from the sound of gunfire. I truly loved firing while flying. The wind in my face, the flash out of the barrel, and the smell of gunpowder just got me going. I will never understand how my fellow mechanics could be content working in the hangar everyday. Heck, I got paid extra for this; I would have done it for free, however, I never told the Army that.

First stop this day, as everyday, was Saigon at pad Hotel 3. We always stopped in Saigon just in case a soldier needed a ride to the Mekong Delta back to his unit. The only way to get around was to catch a Huey. If there was room, they got a ride, simple as that. As we turned final to land, I saw an all too familiar sight, one I shall never forget. Just beside the taxiway were the coolers, an outside morgue, if you will. Right beside them were the metal temporary coffins. This was a much too busy place—there were always warm ones going in and cold ones going out, for the war was over for these brave young men. We couldn't dwell on these things, but of course, the thought was always in the back of our minds. I've delivered some of my fellow Americans to this sight, and it really sucked. Well, time to fly not to dwell. Once we "pulled pitch," our senses focused on flying and not on getting shot.

After leaving Saigon, it was about a one-hour flight to our first stop, a firebase—we had everything from radios to mail to deliver. We climbed to about 4,000 feet and got some refreshing cool air. The gunner and I were always in the turbulent air by virtue of where we sat. We were always putting on our armor and taking it off to put on our jackets. At altitude, we sat on our chicken plates (one inch armor chest plate) so as not to take a bullet up the ass, a common wound when flying high.

Suddenly, Bullet called me on the intercom and said, "Hey, Chief, you want to fly?"

I replied, "You bet."

"Good, because I want to shoot the gun."

So while we were flying, I stepped out on the skid and swung around to the cargo area while Bullet was stepping between the two pilots' seats to take my place. If you could have seen the expression on Mr. Tibbs' face while all of this was going on, it would have been worth a Pulitzer Prize.

I got buckled in and grinned at Peter Pilot and told him, "I have the controls."

He acknowledged, and off I went, flying south and having a ball. Bullet, on the other hand, was having his own fun; he yelled, "Keep her straight, Chief," and he let out a 50-round burst. We both were grinning ear to ear. Mr. Tibbs was not smiling; they never told him about this stunt at flight school.

I flew for about 30 minutes and we traded back. When Bullet got back into his seat, he told Mr. Tibbs that I flew better than he did. It just wasn't fun being the new guy, not to mention the only one on this aircraft. Bullet believed that all crew chiefs should be able to fly, and more importantly, to land. There had been instances when the crew chief had to land or assist the pilot in landing due to both pilots being shot up. Good idea, whatever it takes to get us all home.

We dropped our supplies and headed out for Vinh Long for fuel and lunch. While refueling, a gunship came in behind us and was taking on fuel and rockets. He had some battle damage to the front of his chopper, and the crew chief was hosing blood and such off the windshield. He had punched his rockets into the VC (Viet Cong) on a hill during close air support of the infantry. When he pulled up, he flew into what he had just destroyed. When Bullet saw this, he was fit to be tied. He had tried to get into gunships since he had arrived. He was one of the best pilots I had ever flown with, and he would have been well suited for gun duty, being that he was good and crazy. You have to be both to fly guns every day.

We shut down for lunch and ate with the Navy Seals. We had done insertions into Cambodia with these strange fellows, and they invited us to eat with them anytime. No other Army guys I knew had been invited to break bread with them.

It had to do with respect because we had to volunteer to take them into Cambodia. We had to wear civilian clothes and had no identification on us. If we were to go down, then we would have had to make it to the border on our own to get pulled out. Bullet and I loved the cloak and dagger stuff. We both believed that if there was a golden bullet out there with our name on it, did it really matter what jungle we were in when we bought it?

After lunch, we flew our last sortie to the "cement plant." It was a rock quarry of sorts, except this was one of the places we went in hot. We would stay locked and loaded throughout the landing and takeoff due to some VC who often would dispense a couple dozen rounds at us in hopes he could bag a Huey and four GIs. So, we did not mess around there. We landed, dropped our cargo and got out fast. On the way out, Dick and I would always pop off a few dozen rounds of our own just to keep the bad guys on their toes.

After refueling, we headed for home. It was an uneventful and beautiful day for flying. We made our final stop in Saigon to see if anyone needed a ride home. Some of the metal coffins had been moved, so I knew some of my comrades were on their way home. We pulled pitch and climbed to 2,000 feet and just relaxed a bit, thinking of the great Halloween Party. I could already taste those steaks and cold beer.

It was starting to get dark, we would be home in about 20 minutes. We had started to come down in altitude a little to avoid clouds. Dick and I got our guns ready, for we were getting within .30 cal. range. Suddenly, there was a tremendous explosion. The Huey dropped so fast that I came out of my seat until my belt snapped me back. The aircraft yawed to the left and started to roll over. Bullet grabbed the controls and Peter Pilot keyed the radio, and said "Mayday! Mayday! Satellite 318, 10 klicks east of Saigon, going down, on fire."

I didn't have time to think. I looked at the cockpit and saw more caution lights and bells going off with a big red FIRE! light right in the middle of the instrument panel. I figured we'd been hit by a missile. I stowed my machine gun and looked to the rear of my bird and saw nothing but smoke and flames. We were falling like a greased brick, and the ground was coming up fast. I grabbed my seat belt and pulled it as tight as I could. We were in full autorotation, and it was all in the hands of Bullet—a good pilot, and if we had to go down, he was the pilot I wanted at the controls. I kept my eyes straight ahead and waited for the impact. I thought about getting pinned in the wreckage and burning up. I thought about getting the guns out after impact, to be ready for the bad guys who bagged us. It was weird, I didn't think about dying or home, just survival. The quick and the dead is all you find on the battlefield. I was quick!

Bullet flared the Huey and we started to slow; then we hit, bounced back into the air and hit again. This time the skids collapsed, and the Huey skidded forward across a road and into a small tree, breaking the glass in the front of the helicopter. I jumped out, jettisoned Bullet's door, moved his armor back. I yelled we were on fire, and he unbuckled. I grabbed him by his collar and pulled him out of the cockpit. I ran to the other side, and by now Peter Pilot had gotten out. I went to check on my gunner, and he was lying on the ground away from the Huey. My heart sank, I had never lost a crewman on my bird, and the thought of it was not setting well with me.

He was okay, just terrified and thinking about going into shock. Dick was sobbing; this was his third crash in as many months. He had earned the right to sob. I told him he was a jinx; the only reason I would fly with him was because he could shoot a gnat's ass at 1,000 feet and 90 knots. Dick smiled and we kind of hugged, and then we went to work. We had to decide if we were going to haul ass or stay put. Three helicopters then came on scene to provide medical evacuation or fire support should the bad guys be coming. We ended up unhurt, just shaken a little. We never bugged Peter Pilot again. He was not a cherry anymore, and he had performed well. He got the mayday call out just as he was trained, and help had showed up within minutes.

We missed our party, the strippers, and the beer because we had to spend the night with the helicopter. The next day, we were lifted out by a CH-47, helicopter and all, and then we all got drunk. We got cleared by the shrink to fly again, and we went to Saigon to get a new helicopter. We missed only two days of flying after our accident. We will all remember October 31, 1970, as a day all our skills came together to survive.

No moral to the story and no regrets.

✦ By Larry Harty
   Huey318, RVN 1970–1971, 67N crew chief, U. S. Army Aviation

Larry Harty was a 19-year-old Huey crew chief with the United States Army's 2nd Signal Group, 1st Signal Brigade, in Long Thanh North, from 1970 to 1971. After 23 years in Army Aviation, Harty retired as a master sergeant in 1993.

Larry Harty's poem "Thank You, Ma'am," dedicated to the women who served during the Vietnam War, is published in *Angels in Vietnam: Women Who Served*. Read more adventures of Bullet, Mr. Tibbs, and Larry Harty in Harty's story in this book, "Donut Dollies," chapter 9.

Note: "Ash and trash" as used in the story above is slang for mission flights involving the transporting of soldiers and/or supplies.

Flight Facts: Approximately 12,000 helicopters were used in Vietnam. Some of the several types included the Hughes OH-6A Cayuse "Loach," a light observation helicopter used for command and control, observation, target acquisition, and reconnaissance; the OH-13 Sioux and the OH-23 Raven were light observation helicopters; the CH-47 Chinook; the Marine Corps' CH-46 Sea Knight; Bell's OH-58 Kiowa was used for medevac, reconnaissance and target acquisition, and as scouts for the AH-1 Cobra attack gunship; and the CH-54 Tarhe, the large crane. Five thousand of these were lost in the war. Names such as Shawnee, Mohave, Choctaw, Chicasaw, Seahorse, Sea King, and Seasprite will forever bring back rotary-winged memories for thousands of crew members who flew and died in these amazing machines.

CHAPTER 6

Huey Down

A helicopter does not want to fly.
It is maintained in the air by a variety of forces and
controls working in opposition to each other,
and if there is any disturbance in this delicate balance
the helicopter stops flying—immediately and disastrously.

Harry Reasoner, 1923–1991

Amazing Machines

Helicopters are pretty amazing flying machines. They are so much fun when everything is working right and in synchronization. But let just one little thing go hay-whacky and BAM! Your life just got worse.

✦ Pat Kenny, Semper fi
  HMM-364 Purple Foxes, http://www.hmm-364.org/
  April 1970–April 1971, Vietnam, USMC, helicopter pilot
  Marble Mountain Air Facility, I Corps

Pat Kenny was 24 when he served in Vietnam as a Marine CH-46 Sea Knight helicopter pilot. Today, he is the boat captain of his own fishing guide service on the Columbia River in Richland, Washington. Kenny's tribute "To the Nurses" is published in *Angels in Vietnam: Women Who Served*. See Pat Kenny's "Rules to Live By," chapter 12 in this book.

📖

59

Winged Wisdom

⅓ A fire takes precedence over everything else.
⅓ Pay close attention when someone is telling you
how he survived an emergency situation.

Two-One! You're On Fire!

"Two-One! You're on fire!"

Those were the last words I heard before we crashed. I was a door gunner on a UH-1D Huey Helicopter, tail number 66-00936, in Vietnam. The date was September 26, 1968.

I had been in country for about three months at the time. I was assigned to D Troop, 3rd Squadron of the 5th Cavalry attached to the 9th Infantry Division. Our base was located at Dong Tam in the Mekong River Delta. My aircraft commander, Lieutenant Jim Clary, was a great guy who taught me that officers are just regular guys, too. On the ground it was "Jim," but in the air it was, "Yes, Sir" or "No, Sir." We knew who the boss was. My crew chief, Charles Roberts, was older than most of the guys in the troop, and he really knew his helicopters. We usually had different copilots, also called "Peter Pilots" or just "Petes," from day to day. This day our Pete was WO1 (Warrant Officer 1) Mike Chapas. As I said, I was the door gunner—just a young 20-year-old from a small town in the Panhandle of Texas.

That morning we had been flying a "sniffer" mission without much luck locating any VC (Viet Cong). So our troop air mission commander (AMC), who was also the unit executive officer or XO, Captain Whitworth, ordered us to support some ground troops from the 9th Division. This usually meant we had to circle at 1,000 feet and wait, which was pretty boring. But as soon as we got to the area of operation, there was a call for a medevac. Lt. Clary never hesitated a second when a ground commander asked for a medevac. He was on the radio answering the call, "This is Long Knife Two-One, we have it."

As we got closer to the LZ (landing zone), Lt. Clary told me enemy fire would be on my side of the helicopter, and the LZ was very hot. As I looked down, I could see a helicopter with a big red cross on it turned over on its side. I knew we were going to take a lot of fire. As soon as we started down and I could see the tree line, I started firing my M-60 machine gun. We hit the LZ and the ground troops headed to our aircraft with a guy that was hit bad; he had a chest wound. No fire was received, so I jumped out to help lift him into our copter. We hovered over to another area, and this one was hot, too. We were getting a lot of fire. A staff sergeant (SSG) with a neck wound jumped on, and then I heard one of our pilots say, "I'm hit! You got it!"

We took off and were moving pretty fast, but we weren't climbing. Then I heard someone scream on the radio, "Two-One! You're on fire!"

A second later I saw the sky, then the rice paddy, and then the helicopter flew right over me. I was sure it was falling on top of me. I had not yet buckled my seat belt, and I was thrown out of the ship. The next thing I remember was seeing our helicopter turned upside down and burning. I was about 100 feet from it. Then the fire just went out. I raised up and received enemy fire before I could get back down. I took a hit in the lower right part of my chicken plate (bulletproof vest) that turned me, then I felt a burn in my back. I thought for sure I was the only one alive, and now I was hit.

Soon I heard Lt. Clary call my name, "Hutch!"

I answered with, "I'm here!"

"Are you OK?"

"Yes, Sir."

"Then get over here."

The sound of Lt. Clary's voice came from the other side of the chopper, so I started to crawl toward our downed ship. About 25 feet from my side of the chopper, I found a black soldier with a chest wound. I thought, "This isn't the guy I helped lift in the ship! Where did this guy come from? He must have been loaded on from Roberts' side."

I asked if he could move, and he didn't say a word, then he just took hold of my arm and said, "Help me." I started pulling him along with me, but soon he realized he had to help himself some. This guy was over 200 pounds, and I was around 140 pounds. We finally made it to Lt. Clary's location.

I looked at everyone and could see Roberts was in a lot of pain. Mr. Chapas was in pretty good shape, but he had taken some metal in his leg. Lt. Clary had a very bad foot wound, and there was the other man with the chest wound. He was talking and I could tell he was hurting.

The SSG with the neck wound looked OK, but he wasn't helping the other guys too much. Maybe he was in shock? Lt. Clary asked if I was OK again, and I said, "I'm fine, but I think I was hit in the back." He lifted my shirt and told me I was hit but not bad.

Jim said, "OK, guys, we need to get away from this chopper, so let's start moving back." We were still receiving some fire from the tree line about 200 feet to our front. "There is a hooch over there, so let's go that way."

About halfway to the hooch, Mike Chapas asked Jim if he had the emergency radio.

Jim said, "No!"

Mike said, "I'll go back and get it."

I told Jim I'd better go too and get one of the M-60s. Mike and I got back to the chopper, and when I started to pull off the M-60, we started to take a lot of ground fire. We were still able to get the radio and the gun. I also grabbed a grenade.

After we rejoined the group, Jim took the grenade and rolled it into the hooch. This was a good way of making sure there weren't any VC waiting for us inside. I set the gun up but soon realized that it wouldn't fire because of damage it had received during the crash. I was hoping to get off a few rounds just to let the VC know we had some firepower—maybe keep them off our backs for a while. Only a few months before, one of our Loachs (OH-6 Cayuse helicopter) was shot down. Before the troop could get the pilot and gunner out, they had been over-run and killed by the enemy. I knew this could happen to us.

Jim made radio contact, and soon I saw the C&C (command and control) ship start to come in to get us, but they pulled up. Later, I heard they had taken hits and were forced to land in a rice paddy not too far from us. I saw one Loach fly by, but it also left the area. I then realized it was too hot for any of our guys to get in and get us out. That was when I started to worry. When our Loach pilots, like Ace Cozzalio, stayed out of the area, it was hot! Ace had been put in for the Medal of Honor, which was downgraded to the Distinguished Service Cross for some reason. I can say Ace was the bravest man I ever knew.

It was late in the day, and I knew if we didn't get picked up by nightfall, we did-n't have much of a chance. The VC would wait till dark, then make their move on us. All we had for weapons were four pistols, two .45s and two .38s, which weren't much defense. The two guys with chest wounds couldn't last much longer.

Jim told us he used the emergency radio to call in an air strike. It was on its way! Soon, I watched this Air Force jet drop his load. We were so close I could see the pilot inside the cockpit. I was told later he dropped two 500-pounders, but one was a dud. Whatever he dropped, it did the trick, and none too soon.

It was now sunset. Jim told us to get ready—a chopper was on its way to pick us up, and we needed to load fast. This would be our only chance.

I heard the chopper coming in, and so did the VC. Just as the chopper landed, the VCs started shooting. Mr. Lake was flying UH-lD-00938 with two of my buddies: Crew Chief Mike McGuire and Door Gunner Jim Driver were there to pick us up. We really loaded fast as Mike and Jim covered us with their M-60s firing away. I even started firing my .38 into the tree line.

I will never forget my days as a door gunner for the Long Knives in D Troop 3/5 Air Cav. When I arrived in country we had five UH-lD Hueys: 66-16480, and four sister ships, 66-00936,-00937,-00938, and-00939. All were lost within nine months due to combat damage or on a combat mission: 66-00936, shot down September 26,1968, on a medevac mission; 66-00937, crashed August l968 due to tail rotor failure while on a sniffer mission; 66-16480, shot down October18, 1968, while on a medevac; 66-00938, blown up from a grenade in the fuel tank, March 1969; 66-00939, hit with mortar or rocket, March 1969.

I ETSed (honorable discharge, Expiration of Term of Service) from the Army in December1969 and went to work for Bell Helicopter Company in Amarillo, Texas. Amarillo was Bell's overhaul factory. One morning I was walking up the line, and for some reason I stopped and looked at the data plate on this ship. I read the number 66-00938. This was Mike McGuire's old ship. The ship that had been used to save my life.

+ By Johnny Hutcherson
  Long Knife door gunner, Vietnam, 1968–1969
  D Troop, 3rd Squadron, 5th Cavalry Regiment, (Recon for the 9th Inf. Div.)
  http://www.vhpamuseum.org/5thcav/3rdsquad/3rdsquaddtroop.html

Johnny Hutcherson has been married to Theresa since 1966, before he was drafted. They have four children, Brannon, Heather, Johnna, and Dustin. Hutcherson is retired from Sikorsky Helicopter Co. and lives in Floresville, Texas. Johnny Hutcherson's poem "Do You Know" is published in *Angels in Vietnam: Women Who Served*.

I feel that I used the word "I" too much in my story, and I want to make it very clear, I am not a hero. I was just a young kid of 20 years old and full of fear. However, I did serve with many heroes in Vietnam. Sometimes I wonder why God put me in D Troop 3rd of the 5th Air Cavalry, as D troop was made up of many of the bravest men on earth. My job as a door gunner was to protect the helicopter and support the infantry. I only wish I would have done a better job.

Today I live in Floresville, Texas, with my wife of 36 years. I feel my wife, Theresa, is a Vietnam veteran also. We were married before I went into the Army. She has lived with the effects and deep feelings that the Vietnam War left with me. She has suffered greatly because of me. However, she stayed with me and fought for me. I once heard her ask a VA doctor, "Can you give me back that sweet boy I married before he was sent to Vietnam?" + Johnny Hutcherson

Flight Facts: A "sniffer" mission was a helicopter (a UH-1) search for the enemy using a metal box with a probe for detecting ammonia. A specially-trained soldier came along to operate the cabinet-sized machine and to interpret the information, relaying it to the pilots. The crew chief or door gunner dropped smoke to mark the spot determined by the sniffer. An OH-6 flying behind the UH-1 checked out the marked area. If the Scout crew of the OH-6 saw enemy movement or if the sniffer reading was high, reconnaissance infantry troops were inserted. Or, if the enemy fired on the helicopters, they called in a gunship (such as an AH-1G Cobra) to make a gun run, laying fire on the marked enemy spot.

📖

We Are Just on Loan

It was just another day in Viet Nam for our Huey crew, not knowing today we would be picked up with a shovel. This would be our last time to fly, for today we were to die.

We flew low in the Viet Nam sky, radio played "Harper Valley P.T.A." Then a call we heard, a soldier was hit below. "This is Two One we have it," the pilot said. "Red smoke in site at two o'clock." Rotor blades popped as the pilot banked right. This LZ is Hot!

The gunners fire as metal of death hits our Huey. "I'm hit," the pilot cried as he tried to fly. A voice was heard from above, "Two-One, you're on FIRE"! Our Huey crashes in a big flame, our final day had come.

We were put in a rubber bag and sent home. Our loved ones received a box covered with a flag. For many years we had no place to go. But as for me, in 1982 I found a home, on a black wall made of stone in Washington, D.C. There I waited to see you and the son you carried for me.

One hot day in 1984 you came to touch my name; I heard you tell my son there with you, that this is your dad. He is big and in his teens, looks like me; he has the same color of hair and eyes I once had, this I can see, plus my ears. You are still so pretty and full of life. No please don't cry! You know I never could stand to see your tears. Who is that guy with you, holding your hand? Your wedding band is not the oneI bought you. Oh, I see now, you have a new man. You know that's good, it's ok with me. I can see he is a kind man and cares for you and our son.

I know you have to go, it's getting dark. I hope all of you come back some day. Don't worry about me, I'm here with my crew. I am never alone. There are many of us fly-boys here my dear.

Some were picked up with a shovel like me. Some were washed from their Huey with a hose. That's the way it was to be you know. So please move on and let me go. I was put on earth only as a loan, to you from GOD. We are all just on loan, for someday GOD calls us all home.

✝ By Johnny Hutcherson

📖

For All Our Brothers Who Fell From the Sky

For Roger Herrick and his brother, Capt. Jim Herrick, USAF, MIA

> Darkness falls without a sound
> that mortal ears will ever hear,
> a black lace curtain, swirling down,
> the falling of a crystal tear.
>
> So quick it cuts away the sun,
> a teardrop on a candle flame,
> and darkness comes to mark the place
> that's empty now but for a name.
>
> But many times
> 'tween dusk and dawn,
> half-hidden in the early mist,
> we think of you as you once were,
> bright and laughing, sunlight kissed.

✝ By James M. Hopkins

Mike (James M. Hopkins) wrote this poem for Roger Herrick in tribute to Roger's oldest brother, James, who is still MIA. He was an Air Force pilot, captain, and his plane crashed in Laos on October 27, 1969. Even though James was a fixed wing pilot, I think this can extend to all who flew the "skies of War." + Deanna Gail Shlee Hopkins *Life's Flavors,* http://gecko.gc.maricopa.edu/~dgshleeh/dsstorie.htm

See "Whirling Blades" by James M. Hopkins, chapter 2.

📖

Winged Wisdom

ʚ Never criticize someone else for being FUBAR;
one day you may be Fowled Up Beyond All Recognition.

The Midair

On 4 October 1968, I was involved in a midair collision with an AH-1G XX488 (Cobra). We were cruising along at an altitude of 2,000 feet, returning from a people-sniffer mission (see explanation of "sniffer mission," chapter 6) along the Cambodian border north of Tay Ninh. The mission was complete and we were en route back to Cu Chi. My ship, UHIC-XX210 (Huey), was the lead ship of the fire team.

The AH-1G eased into a formation with us. His blades were under ours, and they were extremely close to our rocket pods, probably within three feet and way too close for comfort. I complained about it, and our aircraft commander, CWO (Chief Warrant Officer) Robert "Hayne" Moore, told him to back off. He slid out to the right, and his blades came up and locked up with ours when he tried to do a wingover as he was leaving. He had misjudged the distance by about a foot. There was a tremendous BANG! when the blades contacted each other. The last I saw of the AH-1G he was in an inverted position going in excess of 100 knots and heading down.

The vibration in my ship was extremely intense, at least a ten-to-one vertical vibration. I looked out of the door and the trees looked about a quarter of an inch tall. I looked over the pilot's shoulder, the master control panel was lit up like a Christmas tree, and nothing was working. I said very loudly, "OH, F***!"

On the intercom, the copilot, WO Ralph "Nolan" Little, was screaming, "Mayday, mayday, we are ALL going to die."

I told them, "Shut up! I don't want to hear about it."

It was all the pilots could do, with both of them on the controls, just to keep the nose up. The vibration continued to worsen, and one machine gun vibrated off its mount and departed the aircraft. Our M-16 assault rifles that were hanging on the pilots' seats vibrated off and disappeared out the cargo door. My gunners and my ammo cans with 2,000 rounds of M-60 ammunition each went out the cargo door.

The altitude was decreasing and the airspeed increasing. My adrenaline level was through the roof. It was just a matter of seconds and it would be over. I was going to die and watch it happen. Visions of sheer terror ran through my mind: images of an explosion on impact and burned to death, and I was helpless to do anything about it. I felt like a caged rat.

I had already made up my mind that if at 60 feet the pilots didn't have control of this thing, I was leaving. I was not Captain Ahab, I didn't have to go down with this ship. I would take my chances hitting the rice paddies below. The vibration intensified further as the altitude decreased; the compartment door on the outer wall where I kept my pistol and camera vibrated off. The pistol and camera disappeared out the cargo door. At about 100 feet, as I was preparing to unbuckle my monkey strap and find a soft spot in the rice below, the pilots somehow got the nose up and flared the ship some. The vibration intensified further as the flare increased, and my helmet was shaken off my head. In a snap judgment that I would live or die with, I had to make a decision—the pilots had it flared, the nose was up, and the airspeed was diminishing, there was water and mud below, and I chose to ride it down.

The pilots pulled all the pitch at 30 feet, and the ship shook violently as we settled and splashed in the rice paddy. We bounced once and we stopped. Somehow we were still upright. Mr. Moore tried to get out, and I grabbed him around the neck and told him to sit still until the blades stop splashing in the rice paddy. It would be a shame to get decapitated with the main rotor blade after doing a spectacular job getting us down. The blades were striking about 10 feet outside the door, causing mud to almost explode from the rice paddy. Every time they hit the water and mud, it tilted the aircraft. When the aircraft finally stopped moving, we exited and set up a small perimeter. Some perimeter: two pistols the pilot had, and one M-60 with about six rounds that were still left in my gunner Specialist Jimmy Cardin's gun. The rest had gone out the door on the way down.

My nerves were shattered, but other than that, I was unscathed physically. An OH-6 was orbiting overhead for security 10 minutes later. A Little Bear slick, from our sister company, came and picked us up.

I went over the ship when it was pipe-smoked (with a CH-47) back in from the field. The transmission mounts were sheered off. The tail boom mounting bolts were badly stress-fractured and it is a wonder it had stayed on, the 42% gearbox was missing, the driveline was snapped. All that held the rotor system on was the lift link bolt, and it was half sheared. I have no idea why it didn't fail. If it had, we would have fallen 2,000 feet to a fiery death.

After this incident, my nerves were fried. Mentally, I couldn't fly any longer. I had nightmares for weeks on end and kept a steady schedule with the chaplain. I chose to work in the mess hall as a cook.

I had been in the mess hall for several weeks, when at three in the morning a 122mm rocket landed a direct hit in the mess hall, blowing it all to hell with me in it. Enough of this! I decided I would rather die flying than be a sitting duck in the mess hall. I think it was the aiming point for every rocket in Southeast Asia.

In the beginning, I substituted on the counter mortar team to just ease back into it. By December I was back into a regular schedule of flying once again, although I was very apprehensive. It was still better than being a sitting duck for the nightly rocket and mortar attacks.

Thirty-three years later, at times late at night I find myself still in that aircraft. Maybe one day I too will get to come home, or it will crash and kill me, and finally it will be over.

✛ By Ron Leonard
  Diamondhead 085, March1968–April 1969, Cu Chi, Vietnam
  25th Aviation Battalion, 25th Infantry Division, http://25thaviation.org

Ron Leonard is the webmaster for the 25th Aviation Battalion. As a crew chief of the UH-1C gunship during the Vietnam War, he was "shot down once, and survived a midair collision 2,000 feet up." He received a Purple Heart, two Distinguished Flying Crosses, the Vietnamese Cross of Gallantry, ten air medals, and several other VietnamWar-related medals.

Leonard is now "in the process of reconstructing the 25th Aviation Battalion's history from the day we left Hawaii until the last man went home. Every day, every battle, every hour." Visit http://25thaviation.org

See Ron Leonard's poem "The Sky" and story "The Last Ride," chapter 14.

📖

Flight Facts: AH-1 Cobra helicopters flew 1,038,969 hours in the Vietnam War. Bell Helicopter specially designed the Cobra to play a direct-fire support role in combat. The UH-1 Huey had been modified as an armed helicopter, but the additional weight and drag created by the weaponry left something to be desired in attack helicopter performance. The addition of the Cobra in 1967 provided extra fire support for the scout, troop, and cargo helicopters.

In 1984, the military began replacing the Cobra, which retired from the Army the end of 2000, with the AH-64 Apache attack helicopters (acquired from Hughes/McDonnell Douglas by Boeing in 1997). Today, Apache pilots continue to fly in combat and peace-keeping operations in hot spots around the world such as Bosnia, Korea, and Iraq.

In 2006, the Army will add the next generation's attack helicopter, the Comanche by Boeing and Sikorsky Aircraft Corp., designed for reconnaissance and as an attack helicopter, to its 21st century inventory.

The Saddest Day of My Life

March 15,1975, my 28th birthday, turned out to be the saddest day of my life. I lost four very close friends that day: CW2 (Chief Warrant Officer 2) John C. Johnson, WO1 (Warrant Officer 1) Desmond P. Downey, Specialist 5 Harvey Salas, and Specialist 5 Earl Rankhorn. All of these men were on a medevac rescue mission out of Schweinfurt, Germany, to pick up four injured solders who had been seriously hurt in a jeep wreck.

A little after 4 a.m., I received a call from the Charge of Quarters at the unit. He told me to get to the unit ASAP because there was an emergency in progress. I didn't know what it was until I arrived at the hangar and found out that aircraft 15739 was missing. Another four-man crew, two pilots and two specialists, had been in the air searching and praying to sight an aerial flare from one of the crew members of the downed helicopter.

My crew took off shortly after them, and we flew around for an hour and a half with no luck. Finally, one of the pilots from the other airborne helicopter spotted a fire and called on us to check it out. He couldn't land because he was low on fuel.

It was still dark as we circled over the small fire. Then, I saw the tailboom of the aircraft; it had broken off in the crash. I knew it was going to be a bad one.

The pilot found a clearing and landed. Three of us jumped out of the helicopter and started running toward the crash. We were yelling out some of the missing crew members' names. When we got to the still-smoldering wreck, we counted four bodies, all dead.

We secured and tied down our aircraft. Then we prepared a landing zone for other helicopters that might come out to the crash site. It was two to three hours later before another helicopter started to circle around the area, looking for a place to land. We fired off flares so that the circling pilot could see us. We guided him in, and he dropped off two military police from Schweinfurt to secure the crash site.

About 1500 hours, the rest of the investigation board arrived at the scene. They looked at the wreckage and released the bodies. About 6 p.m. we finally left the area and returned to Schweinfurt, Germany. We were physically and emotionally exhausted. The 2nd Platoon, 421st Medical Company would never be the same after that day.

I had switched duties with my buddy and fellow flight medic, Harvey Salas, so I could have my birthday off on March 15. He had a date, but said that missing one date would not kill him—it did, and he died in my place. I will never forget that night, and I relive it on my birthday every year. Fate also put me on the search and rescue that found what was left—that hurt even worse. But, I stayed with him and my fellow crew members until the mortuary picked up the remains at the crash site.

They are in my prayers every day. Four good men gone! Why? Only God knows.

✝ By Doc Larry D. Kimmith
Combat Medic/Flight Medic
Doc Larry, http://www.geocities.com/dustoff739

Larry D. Kimmith, "Dustoff 739," served three and a half years in Vietnam, 1966–1970, as a combat medic with the 2nd Battalion, 27th Infantry Regiment Wolfhounds in Cu Chi; the 94th Medical Detachment, Camp Holloway Dispensary, near Pleiku; 755th Medical Detachment, 170th Assault Helicopter Company, Pleiku; and the 85th Evacuation Hospital in Phu Bai (moved from Qui Nhon, November 1968).

From November12, 1974, to June 8, 1977, with 2nd Platoon, 421st Medical Company (Air Ambulance), Kimmith flew 133 Dustoff missions, attending more than 140 patients. March 15, 1975, is the one mission he'll never forget.

The Huey helicopter lost in the crash that day was UH-1H, tail number 68-15739.

A Wife's View

It still makes me sad. I see their faces. My heart laughs at the sight of them the last time I saw them. Playing pool and eating my homemade bread. Laughing and cutting up. Having fun.

My heart cries when I remember the way my husband was called to the base. Little did he (we) know that it was a rescue mission on four of our best friends. Downey (WO1 Desmond P. Downey) had just come back from vacation. We had helped him paint his place because his bride-to-be would be here in two weeks and we wanted everything just perfect. Earl (Spc. 5 Earl Rankhorn) was the type of person who always was laughing or smiling. You could hear his deep laugh throughout the whole building. Earl was about to be a father. The other two (CW2 John C. Johnson and Spc. 5 Harvey Salas) had plans also, but put them on hold to do their duty. Time for them was short.

For the ones left behind, the time we had shared with them was precious. We are so glad that the times we had were joyful.

Sometimes I hear someone laugh and I turn around to look. For a moment, I forget, but only for a moment. I knew my husband left early that morning. I found out about the accident on the radio when I was in the process of making my husband's birthday cake. The radio said that a 421st Medevac helicopter crashed early, and all members were believed to be dead. Names being withheld pending notification of family. None of the wives found out who it was until the men came back from the mission (about 6:30 p.m.).

As a wife, I (we) went through a lot of pain. The pain is as real today as it was on March 15, 1975. The sounds of the past, the times we went to the movies, played pool, all the things friends do together. As a group, we all became close and seemed more like family—as I think about that time in my life, my heart cries.

A wife's view is a little different. When Larry and the guys came back, they didn't look tired—they looked like the walking dead. Life was drained from Larry's face. The steps he took were out of habit, not from a conscious effort. He walked past me like I wasn't even there. There is one thing Larry didn't tell. Early on the morning of March 15th Larry woke up screaming, "They're going down! They're going down!" I told him it was okay. It was only a bad dream. I reached to turn off the light. As I did, I looked at the clock. It was 2:10 a.m. When Larry got to the crash site and found Downey, he noticed Downey's watch. It had stopped at 2:10 a.m.

I still miss those guys. I haven't had the desire to bake homemade bread, cookies, or cakes since.

✦ By Mary A. Smith

📖

Flight Facts: According to statistics compiled by the United States Army Safety Program, 35 service members lost their lives in Army-related helicopter accidents in 1975. Each year, men and women die in military helicopter crashes. Each death—sobering and shocking—changes the lives of families, friends, and co-workers forever. Those of us who have known someone taken suddenly and tragically in a helicopter, salute their lives in our hearts and memories.

CHAPTER 7

War Memories

It is possible to fly without motors,
but not without knowledge and skill.

Wilbur Wright, 1867–1912

Air Assault

Thumping down the valley floor,
contour flying—open door.

Squadron's choppers in a line,
the Air Assault goes in on time.

Heart is pumping—temples too,
Cobra Gunships—standing to.

Carabiner locked in place,
try to hide my fearful face.

Check my bag and check my rope,
God give me some bloody hope.

Rifle slung behind my back,
Grenades and ammo in my pack.

Machine gun belts cut in my neck,
join the Gun Group on the deck.

Two fingers up—two minute test,
check my kit and do my best.

Chopper flaring—out the door,
stand on skids and count to four.

Throw my bag—back and behind,
Go! Go! Go!—you're on the line.

Thumb up bum—rappel to earth,
clear the line and hit the dirt.

Pull the pack strap roll away,
God just get me through this day.

✦ By Mike Subritzky
   Sergeant, 161 Battery, Royal New Zealand Artillery

Born in Kati Kati, New Zealand, Mike Subritzky served in the Royal New Zealand Navy, Royal New Zealand Artillery, Royal New Zealand Air Force, U.S. Navy-Task Force 43 Antarctica, and Polish (Independent) Reserve Brigade. Although he did not go to Vietnam, Subritzky is no stranger to war with 13 tours of duty to his credit, including the Rhodesian war.

As a writer and war poet, Subritzky is able to bring war veterans of all nations together in a common unity of healing, courage, and understanding. Mike Subritzky is the author of several books including his most recent, *The Flak Jacket Collection*. His book *The Vietnam Scrapbook—The Second ANZAC Adventure* was nominated for New Zealand Book of the Year Awards 1996 and named Book of the Quarter by Texas State University April–June 1998. Mike was also honored by the New Zealand ex-Vietnam Services Association by having a copy of his book laid at the Vietnam War Memorial Wall in Washington, D.C. during the 1997 pilgrimage. Mike also received the American Vietnam Veterans (honorary) Distinguished Service Medal 1997, "for his contribution to all veterans of the Asian conflict and immortalizing the Vietnam veterans of New Zealand for all time."—United States Congressional Cold War Citation 2000. His numerous poetry awards have certainly earned him the title of The Kiwi Kipling.

See more of Mike Subritzky's poetry at *The Flak Jacket Collection, New Zealand war poetry*, http://www.geocities.com/mike_subritzky. Mike Subritzky is

the president and co-founder of the *International War Veterans' Poetry Archive,*
http://www.iwvpa.net

📖

The "Dear John"
A Chopper Yarn from the Rhodesian War

In 161 Battery it was a tradition that if any member of the battery got a "Dear
John" while the battery was away anywhere, then that letter was pinned on the
Battery Notice Board and each and every member of the unit wrote back a "Dirty
Bitch" reply to his ex just to let her know that what she had done was a sh**y
thing. And we all hoped that her newfound love gave her terminal herpes.

I think the tradition was begun by the battery in Korea or possibly Vietnam;
in any event, it was continued throughout my time with the Gunners.

On the 6 January 1980, we were deep in the communist-held area of
Operation Tangent when we received our first mail from New Zealand in more
than a month. Amongst the mail was a letter for Stewart Ashworth—a "Dear
John." Ash was pretty pissed off about it for some few days and was down in the
dumps. We Gunners were digging a path out to the chopper pad a couple of days
later while Ash was on stagg (sentry duty). Paul Gregg, Peter McArthur and
myself sat down under a Mopami tree and discussed Ash's love life. We then came
up with a plan to get him a new woman, and the quickest way to do that was perhaps to drop a line to Radio Hauraki in Auckland, New Zealand, and ask them to
put a request out over the radio.

Who knows, Ash might well get a couple of replies.

I pulled out my message pad, and between the three of us we wrote a letter to
the Auckland DJ, Kevin Black, who usually ran the morning breakfast show on
Hauraki. Later that afternoon, Paul assisted Corporal Garven, who was a signaler,
to rig a D10 wire from Lima up to the Police fort. Then, they connected an old
Army-issue telephone at each end. It actually worked, provided you yelled down
the mouthpiece. It was even connected onto the police switchboard. They gave us
the phone number of two short rings (party-line style). Just as a postscript, I
wrote on the bottom of the letter to Kevin Black, "Blackie, if you want to give us
a buzz, our phone number is two short rings on the Mhudlambudzi line." We
wrote "Forces Concession" on the envelope, put it on the next outgoing Scout
chopper, and quietly forgot about it—with no one bothering to tell Ash.

The choppers were really our only contact with the outside world in the early part of the operation as most of the roads in our area had been resowed with mines once we were deployed as peacekeepers in our area of operations. The choppers (Scouts, Pumas, and Gazelles) as well as C-130 airdrops were our lifeblood.

Life continued pretty much each day with stagg, patrolling, medical duty, checking in guerrillas as they entered Lima, plus a host of other tasks that cropped up.

I was also detailed by Major Hewitt to paint a small Kiwi bird and the letter "L" on every chopper that landed at our loc-stat (location of this station). One particular Puma crew's pilot complained, and when he got back to Bulawayo he had his ground crew paint it out. Next time he flew in to our loc-stat, we painted Lima Kiwis not only on the nose of his bird but on the doors as well, and he got the message and left them after that. Pat Hawai, a member of our team, had served in Antarctica, and on the ice the vehicle used by the New Zealanders was called "The Kiwi Express." It featured a Kiwi with a pair of combat boots painted on both sides. We had two Land Rovers at Lima and so I painted one up as the "Kiwi Express No. 1" and the other as "Kiwi Express No. 2." There are several now-famous pics that turn up in various war history books that show Pat and a guerrilla officer in one of these vehicles.

We always ate under a large pink C-130 cargo chute as it was cooler there, and one of the grunts constructed a rifle rack for us to stow our weapons whilst eating meals. That rifle rack became a most important gauge as to the state of stress and danger felt by the team at any given time. If you had been away and something scary had happened, you could always tell at a glance upon your return by simply looking at the rifle rack. If there were weapons stowed on the rack then you could relax, but if it was empty you kept your weapon close to you. It seems humorous now, but we sat playing cards with all participants alert and their personal weapons draped across their knees, but back then it was sometimes very, very intense.

We had a "Claytons" Stand-To every morning at 30 minutes before dawn, and everyone got up and just sat facing outwards with weapons close and in state two (a full magazine placed on a weapon, but not cocked). We were not allowed to dig shell scrapes as they were considered a provocation. We dug bloody big storm water drains instead! From memory, dawn was about 0630.

On the 22 January at about 2100, all hell broke loose at Assembly Place "Kilo" when elements of ZANLA (communist guerillas loyal to their tribal leader Robert Mugabe) and ZIPRA (communist guerillas loyal to their tribal leader, Joshua Ngkomo) had a crack at each other. We were listening to the various contact reports as they came down on our radio net. Things then intensified to a mortar duel between both groups that lasted for quite some time. We were in the fortunate position of being able to monitor the radio traffic from both opposing sides as the various sit-reps (situation reports) came in. The duel finally petered out and next morning when the guys at Kilo sent medics out to check the causalities and bury the dead, nobody had even been scratched. It is amazing really just how much metal it takes to actually kill someone by percentage. On another occasion a platoon of Rhodesian Light Infantry were ambushed by a company of ZANLA, and for a period of more than 30 minutes both sides threw everything but the kitchen sink at each other. The Rhodesians (white soldiers loyal to the legitimate government of Ian Smith) were forced to pull back, and ZANLA captured a Rhodesian GPMG (General Purpose Machine Gun). Casualties for the entire firefight was one Rhodesian troopie hit in the knee by an AK round.

Next morning I was woken at 0530 and told to report to the radio tent, as there was a phone call for me from New Zealand. I stumbled out of my hoochie, not really believing what I had been told, as the phone line only went up to the police fort about two klicks away, and yet I was very concerned for the health of my mother who had emphysema and had been expected to die for some time.

When I picked up the phone I quietly said, "Hello."

A very distant but familiar voice replied, "Is that Sergeant Subritzky?"

I said, "Yes, I am Sergeant Subritzky."

Then a second question, "Are you Sergeant Mike Subritzky who wrote to Radio Hauraki about your mate with the broken heart?"

"Yes," I assured him.

"Excellent, Mike, this is Kevin Black from Radio Hauraki, and you're on the Breakfast Show!"

I couldn't believe it! Somehow or other Blackie had tracked us down to our very tiny corner of Africa, and to this day I am amazed as to just how he did it. We talked for a while and he asked after Ash, and I described Ash to him over the phone. Then he wished us all "Good Luck" and hung up the phone. It was really good to hear from him, as he was a link from home. Unknown to myself, the conversation went out over the airwaves, and my wife, who was working at Raventhorpe Hospital in South Auckland, actually heard it in the ward. The Gunners at 161 Battery were also cleaning their L5s in the Home Bay building and caught the transmission as well.

A couple of weeks later, on the 20 February and just after morning smoko, a Gazelle chopper arrived with Major Hewitt returning from a briefing at either Bulawayo or Salisbury. Onboard the chopper were also three sandbags, jam-packed with scented love letters, all of them addressed to:

Bombardier Stewart Ashworth RNZA
Assembly Place Lima
Operation Tangent
NZATMC Rhodesia
SOUTHERN RHODESIA.

To say that Ash was astounded would be something of an understatement. He quietly excused himself for the rest of the day and retired to his hoochie to read his fan mail. From that day onward he used one of the sandbags (with the more explicit letters) as a pillow.

That night I was on radio stagg and took down the NSR (National Sitrep):

War intensifies as it gets closer to the elections;
Op Hurricane: 3 contacts with 2 casualties in the Rhodesian Security Forces, Greys Scouts deployed;
Op Thrasher: 2 contacts with 2 guerrilla KIAs, land mine initiated with 1 AMA (African male adult) wounded—mine laid in last three days;
Op Repulse: 2 contacts with 2 wounded, 6 FRELIMO (Monzambique guerrillas) surrendered, 1 Swiss priest bayoneted to death, land mine confirmed exploded; Op Grapple: NTR (nothing to report), Op Tangent: NTR.

For us at Lima it was a quiet night on the veldt.

✦ By Sergeant Mike Subritzky
RNZA, Kiwi Peacekeeper, NZATMC AP Lima, Rhodesian War 1979–1980

Read Mike Subritzky's story "Rifleman Down," chapter 8.

Note: "Claytons" Stand-to is New Zealand/Australian military jargon for a derogatory term meaning less than professional. The word "Claytons" comes from a high-priced, top-shelf drink that sold for the exact same price as spirits but in fact had absolutely no alcohol in it. The whole idea was an absolute failure.

A "shell scrape" is a hole in the ground that is 6 feet long, 2 feet wide and 18 inches deep. It is the very first thing that you dig as soon as you stop walking. If the shit hits the fan you dive into it as fast as possible and start talking to Jesus.

"Smoko" is New Zealand/Australian jargon for morning or afternoon tea or coffee break.

"Veldt" is a South African word for the bush, a grassy field with large shade trees. ✦ Mike Subritzky

📖

Flight Facts: The Gazelle is a French-built light-utility helicopter by Eurocopter/Aerospatiale; first flown in 1967. The Puma is a medium-sized helicopter used for troop transport built by Eurocopter in 1987.

Winged Wisdom

☞ When you are fatigued, find the time for a nap.
☞ Find something good to say about folks
who you think are not operating at full RPM.
☞ Watch out for wires.

Dear Bill

My second tour in Vietnam was as an advisor to the Vietnamese Army soldiers at the company level. This time my main ride was an OH-6 LOH (Light Observation Helicopter).

My company was static, protecting a key bridge along Highway 13 in Long Khanh Province. There was little threat in that location, so my brigade senior advisor often used me as an aerial observer for operations throughout the province. WO2 (Warrant Officer 2) Bill Smart was the pilot assigned to the LOH in our AO (area of operations).

We spent many hours together in that mighty little helicopter. Bill often passed the controls to me because of my civilian rating when he was busy navigating. We were quite a team calling for artillery and VNAF (Vietnamese Air Force) Skyraiders while buzzing around the AO like an angry bumblebee. Bill was really smooth with that maneuverable little bird until one day when he almost killed both of us.

I had been out with another company on a night ambush, and Bill came to our location to pick me up. The CO (commanding officer) wanted me to go support another company that was in contact 12 km (kilometers) away. It was a hurry-up mission, and I jumped into the LOH as soon as the skids touched down. Bill began lift-off as soon as I hit the seat. As I was getting strapped in, out of the corner of my eye I saw a wire passing overhead. Without realizing it, Bill had maneuvered us under an overhead power line and it was almost center mast when I saw it.

Another time I would have shouted "wire," but for some unknown reason this time I stayed quiet. The rotors passed between the poles and underneath the wire before Bill pulled pitch for takeoff. Over the intercom I then said, "Uh, Bill, do you realize that you just hovered under those wires right there?"

He turned white as a ghost and began to shake uncontrollably. I took the controls and got us straight and level while he began rambling about a "Dear John" letter he had received from his wife the night before and that he was a ball of knots inside. He settled down after a while; we called in another team to support the contact and returned to base camp. Bill grounded himself after that flight, and since he was within a month of DEROS (date eligible for return from overseas,) he never flew another mission.

✦ By Slim Myers
   Integrity Air, http://www.flyintegrityair.com

Slim Myers served two tours in Vietnam: 1968–1969 as an Artillery forward observer with the 11th Armored Cavalry Regiment, Black Horse, and 1969–1970 as an advisor to the Republic of Vietnam Army. He also served as the battalion commander of "The Big Red One" during Desert Storm. He retired as a lieutenant colonel after 25 years (11 of those years in the 1st Infantry Division, The Big Red One) with the U.S. Army.

Today, Myers is founder and chief executive officer of Integrity Air, which serves the Pikes Peak Region, operating from the Colorado Springs Airport, Colorado Springs, Colorado. Integrity Air, http://www.flyintegrityair.com, provides world-class corporate air charter service for businesses, groups, and individuals.

📖

Winged Wisdom

෪ Some things you do may scare you—
learn to know when it's okay to be scared and
when that fear is a little bell warning you not to do that thing.

Life or Death Decision

In the spring of 1967, in an area about 35 miles northwest of Saigon, I had to make one of the biggest decisions of my life. We had been flying solo missions, mostly supply runs to small encampments of the 1st Infantry Division. The troops were there to slow down the movement of supplies that were coming directly from North Vietnam off the Ho Chi Minh Trail. There had been some fighting, but not nearly as bloody as we had expected it to be. Even though men were getting wounded and killed daily, this was considered a relative pause in the action between much bigger battles that loomed ahead for us.

Our intelligence reports indicated that we should be on the lookout for large movements of both supplies and troops coming into this sector. We had not seen any signs that this was true, but we had been keeping a watchful eye on anything that moved on the ground. We had not received any hostile fire during the morning operations.

My helicopter commander was a major who had just arrived from a tour of several years in Germany. He was a West Point graduate and was a strictly by-the-book style military leader. That was the way he had managed his duties in Germany. He was determined to continue those ways in the Nam. He appeared to me as a real "no nonsense" type of guy with very little sense of humor. When he gave an order, he expected a full 100 percent obedience by those he commanded. He did not want to foster any friendships between himself and us lower ranking souls in the unit. He was in charge, he was "the man," and for those of us who did not outrank him, we were there to support and obey his orders. That was the way things were going to be. We knew he wouldn't be open to any questions or suggestions, we had to do as he said; there was never going to be any debates about what he wanted us to do.

During his first couple of weeks in the Nam, the major was still trying to figure out how to find the LZs (landing zones) and how to read the maps of the area. He did not know the names of places we had to fly to, and he had no clue as to where these places were in relation to other places or to our base camp. Without a map in his hand, this guy wouldn't have any clue to where we were. (The "old guys" who had been there for a while could follow roads and rivers and head toward landmarks such as Black Virgin Mountain.) Yet, he asked very few questions, if any.

On this particular morning, we were flying higher in the sky (over 800 feet) than felt comfortable to me. We were not at our normal treetop-level altitude. The major had an aversion to flying too close to the ground. He did not yet realize the risks that flying at higher altitudes presented. Eventually he would learn—

like all new pilots did—that flying at treetop level was actually much safer. We could sneak up on enemy troops well before they could see or hear us coming; this was the common procedure in Nam—fly low and fast. Keep your profile down close to the ground.

From our more lofty position in the sky, we could see much farther around the countryside. I think it may have been helpful for him in spotting landmarks for his navigation. We did have a greater view of all that was down below, but it also made us an easier target. We were not high enough to avoid small arms fire and not low enough to sneak up on anyone. We just kind of hung in the sky like a big fat, slow moving target.

We were flying just a click (a kilometer or 0.62 of a mile) outside of a small hamlet, when I spotted a group of about 30 people below us who appeared to be moving down the road in a military formation. They were all carrying what looked like some kind of weapon on their shoulders. There also was a man in the front who seemed to be acting as a leader for the group. They were all dressed in the typical black pajamas that the VC (and most everyone living in Nam) wore. Since this was so close to the Ho Chi Minh Trail, it certainly appeared that it could be a good-sized squad of VC (Viet Cong).

The major went into action right away giving orders. He immediately determined that they were VC troops—he had no doubts. He ordered me to fire my M-60 machine gun on the formation below. Now, my M-60 could fire 750 rounds of 7.62 mm of ammo a minute—it would have shredded that group of people in just a matter of a few seconds. I looked down at the formation and thought what he saw was correct, but then I froze. I couldn't pull the trigger on the machine gun. I could not get myself to squeeze off a single round. I was overcome with great apprehension and a feeling that something was not right.

I sat behind my M-60 doing nothing. The major was going crazy and yelling at me. He let me know that he had given me a direct order to fire. It was not optional. But I just sat there, knowing that something was not right with this picture. I told the major I was not going to fire. I had some heavy doubts about what we were seeing down on the road.

The major could not believe that I had actually questioned his orders. He was mad as hell. He told me that I had disobeyed a direct order in combat. That was a punishable offense. He let me know, in no uncertain terms, that he was going to bring me up on charges. Those charges could mean 20 years or more in a military prison at Leavenworth.

I told him that we needed to fly lower. I wanted him to make a pass over the group's formation so we could get a better identification. In the meantime, he had circled the aircraft so that the left door gunner was directly in line to fire his weapon on those on the ground. To my surprise, the door gunner also refused the order to shoot. He showed some exceptional courage by supporting my position. He fully understood what he had just done, and that took my breath away. He was certainly not looking for any trouble from the major, but there he was making a stand with me on this issue. It could have been viewed as a mutiny by the military court system. This was a very serious breach of military law, and we each could have been facing life sentences. I was in awe that he had such courage and conviction, and he was basing it on his belief in my feelings. I hoped to God that I was right, for both of our futures. That was a lot of weight on my shoulders.

The major was debating with the copilot, a young warrant officer from Texas, about calling in an air strike or at least some artillery. The young pilot, who had flown with us many times before, suggested that we take the aircraft down for a closer look. Finally, after what seemed to be a very long time (all of these conversations had happened in less than a minute), we dropped down from our rather higher and awkward altitude and made a descent toward the group of people on the ground. We had our M-60 machine guns at the ready position, aiming right at the heart of the group.

We came down to about 100 feet. We were unsure of what to expect and were ready for all hell to break loose as we passed off to the right side of them. The first clue we had that they might not be the enemy was the fact that they stayed on the road the whole time we were above them. They had not run into the cover of the surrounding jungle. The second big clue was that no one was firing at us as we passed by them at only 100 feet in the air.

As we flew across the road, it became painfully obvious to all of us who they were; this was just a group of school age children with their garden tools, marching in a formation to the community garden. The leader was a priest dressed all in black. My heart raced; I got all emotional and actually felt tears rolling down my face. I realized just how close we had come to killing all these young children.

I couldn't see the major's face, but I imagined that it turned pale. All of us onboard were visibly shaken by this event. The major had given direct orders to both his gunners to kill them all. He even wanted to order an air strike on this group of 30 children. Now, he said very little. I had chills running down my spine and noticed that my hands were shaking.

Why had I and my trusting door gunner both refused to fire? I have no answers. I went with my feelings, which at the time were so very clear and strong that I should not pull the trigger. I risked going to jail because I followed my feelings and not my orders. What if I had been wrong and they were really VC? I had risked the helicopter getting shot down and the life of every crew member— based only on my feelings. I quickly learned in Nam to never question my intuitive feelings. It seemed that those feelings were greatly heightened in combat and dangerous situations. In this case, it saved 30 young children and a priest from being killed. That would have been a major tragedy that I could never have lived with because it would have haunted me for the rest of my life.

The major and I became much better friends after that day. He actually learned to trust those working for him. He began to ask questions and rely on the combat-experienced men around him. He turned out to be a very good human being and a fine officer. He also proved many times over to be a brave and courageous pilot—someone whom I felt confident flying with and risking my own life for. I think we both learned something that day that forever changed the way we looked at life and ourselves.

✦ By Bill McDonald
   The Vietnam Experience, http://www.vietnamexp.com
   LZ Angel, http://www.lzangel.com

"Life or Death Decision" is reprinted here, with permission, from Bill McDonald's book, *A Spiritual Warrior's Journey*. See his stories in this book, "The First Unofficial Bombing Raid of Cambodia" and "All Washed Up in Georgia," chapter 1; and "Answer to a Prayer," chapter 2.

CHAPTER 8

War Canoe to the Rescue

If you are in trouble anywhere in the world,
an airplane can fly over and drop flowers,
but a helicopter can land and save your life.

Igor Sikorsky, 1889–1972

Flight Facts: In April of 1962, the first aeromedical evacuation unit to deploy to Vietnam, the 57th Medical Detachment, arrived in country at Nha Trang, near the 8th Field Hospital. In January of 1963, the unit moved to Tan Son Nuit Air Base in Saigon.

The air ambulances, the first UH-1 Hueys used in combat, blew dust everywhere as they landed in the fields to extract wounded soldiers. The pilots adopted the call sign "Dustoff" as a fitting label for their missions.

Over the next 11 years, until March of 1973, the Dustoff crews of the 57th evacuated more than 100,000 injured troops from combat zones. These air evacuations played a major role in the survival of the injured, contributing to the lowest mortality rate of any American conflict in military history to that point.

The call sign "Medevac," medical evacuation, originated with the 1st Cavalry Division, also during the Vietnam War. Medevac helicopters flew an estimated 500,000 missions during the Vietnam War. These daring rescue crews carried about 900,000 injured soldiers and patients, greatly increasing their survival rate. Thanks to the helicopters, a larger percentage of injured men survived in Vietnam than in previous wars.

Before The Battle

We remember you on Luscombe Field
deep in young men's pensive thought
waiting for the great thumming sound
of the helicopters coming to get you;
the sun bright sharp off the red laterite earth
hurting your eyes as you looked to the horizon,
feeling butterflies of nervous anticipation
two inches below your web belts and knowing that
soon you would be running amongst the smoke and
noise of the landing zone, as the armed
helicopters wheeled on the outer edge of the
maelstrom.

Waiting there on Luscombe Field, ears straining
for the thump thump of rotor blades
and the olive green orbs of the helicopters
suspended low on the glittering horizon—
huge noise in the drumbeat of their engines
wheeling down in great arcs and sheeting dust
as they settle and beckon impatiently
for your young green bodies.

Now lifting you quick and high to the cool bite,
the refreshing rush of air through the open doors
and you not saying much, unable to be heard above
the pounding of the turbine's roar—
but checking for the twentieth time
the fill of your magazines and watching far below
the jungle's rim where a sea of flame marks
the place where you will land.

Your young hearts beating faster as you spiral down
to that moment when the skids touch the earth,
your eyes smarting as you pour from the helicopter
doors, into the sudden assault of rotor driven dust
and cordite—safety catches off, up and running
across the shattered ground, not feeling the cut of

thigh grass as you disappear into the rearing
wall of trees and needle spiked bamboo
crackling in red tracer light as the gunships
make their final pass.

✦ By Lieutenant John A. Moller
    RNZIR, Whiskey Two Company RNZIR, Vietnam 1968–1969

John Moller is a New Zealander who served as a platoon commander with Whiskey Two Company, 4RAR/NZ (Royal Australian Regiment/New Zealand) and 6RAR/NZ (ANZAC—Australian and New Zealand Army Corps) Infantry Battalions during the Vietnam War, 1968–1969.

John is a respected poet and is accredited with having written some of the most thought provoking verse to have come out of the Vietnam conflict. His poetry has been compared with the work of the First World War poets Wilfred Owen and Siegfreid Sassoon. His work is well known internationally and has been used to assist with the treatment of veterans suffering from PTSD (post-traumatic stress disorder).

Upon leaving the New Zealand Army, John has involved himself with veterans' affairs as well as agent orange issues. He is the president of the New Zealand Vietnam Veterans Association. ✦ Mike Subritzky

Read more of John Moller's poetry at *The International War Veterans' Poetry Archives,* http://www.iwvpa.net. Read about him and his book, *The Punji Pit, Poems of the New Zealanders in the Vietnam War,* at http://maori2000.com/moller. Moller's poetry also is published in *Angels in Vietnam: Women Who Served.*

📖

Winged Wisdom

  ᚱ Have your compass re-swung from time to time.
    ᚱ Learn to sleep anywhere you have to.
  ᚱ Don't try to cheat death with wild maneuvers.
  ᚱ Memorize the cockpit instrument limitations.

Rifleman Down

In 1986 I transferred from the Royal New Zealand Artillery, where I worked as a gunnery instructor at the School of Artillery, to the Royal New Zealand Air Force, where I was then employed as a senior instructor at the RNZAF (Royal New Zealand Air Force) General Service Training School.

My new appointment saw me teaching Air Force recruits drill, weapon training, shooting, first aid, rescue techniques, map reading, bushcraft, mountaincraft, survival, and a host of other skills required in the New Zealand Armed Forces. Though I preferred to teach weapon training and shooting, I was usually employed as a drill instructor.

The winter months in New Zealand are June, July, and August. At about the end of June our unit received a squadron's worth of Australian Airfield Defence troopies who were from the 2nd Airfield Defence Squadron, which was based at RAAF (Royal Australian Air Force) Richmond (Sydney) and RAAF Williamstown (Brisbane). The ADGs (Airfield Defence Guards) were considered the elite of the Australian Air Force. Virtually all of them were para-trained, and as well had other skills such as dog handlers and door gunners on choppers. They were highly trained and fit, and I was impressed by their professionalism.

They were with us for about a month, and during that time we trained them at RNZAF Camp "Dip Flat," which is at the base of the snow covered Saint Arnaud mountain range. For the final deployment I was required to take a stick (chopper's worth) of ADGs up to the "tops" (mountain tops) and spend a day teaching them how to build snow caves, pack igloos, and wind trenches. A snow cave simply means that a snow wall or drift is found, and it is then dug into using entrenching tools to make a small entrance. Then, it is widened to accommodate as many soldiers as required.

Pack igloos require a little more skill and planning. Everyone's pack is pushed together to form a hump, and then this is covered over with a thick layer of snow which is then pounded solid. The smallest person in the stick then digs his/her way to the centre and gently removes all of the packs. All members of the stick then burrow inside the igloo, and then the packs are dragged back in. A fair amount of practice is required to get the igloo livable.

A wind trench is used as a last-ditch effort to get all members of the stick below the level of the snow, as the wind at altitude is a killer.

My stick were choppered by a Huey (UH-1D) up to the mountain range to about 6,000 feet early one morning, and I spent the next several hours instructing the Aussie ADGs with me on survival above the snowline. I loved riding in choppers and had flown in them all over the world, although usually with an underslung 105mm L5 (Pack) Howitzer. This ride was simply a survival course.

Most of the men in the stick had never seen snow before, and once the lectures were completed, they spent the rest of the morning making snowmen and throwing snowballs at each other.

About 1400 we had a meal of freeze-dried rations, using snow as the water source. I had been in the area many times before and knew that the walk to Lees Creek was a fairly leisurely walk of about four hours. This meant we should arrive at the hut just after last light, giving the stick a bit of practice at night navigation.

At 1500 we saddled up and began the slog down and off the mountain. Although I knew the area, I still had one of the corporals act as lead scout and map-read the way. It was then that I learned that one of the men in my stick, a sergeant, was in fact not an ADG but rather a fireman from RAAF Garbutt in Townsville. His name was Dan Petty. When I asked him how much jogging he did, I was surprised to learn that he had recently had a heart operation and was still recovering. With this knowledge I informed the stick that we would move below the snowline and spend the night camped at a hut at a place known as Lees Creek. We were all in full battle order complete with basic webbing, packs, and a radio.

I had Dan walk in front of me, and I was in the centre of the stick of seven men. For the first three hours Dan was fine, but with one hour to go it began to snow and the temperature dropped dramatically. We took Dan's webbing, rifle, and pack and redistributed them amongst us, and as well got him eating "sparkles" (a sweet full of energy and sugar). With about 30 minutes to go to the hut, Dan began to show the first signs of hypothermia and began shivering. We were now off the mountain and in amongst beech trees that were clearly blazed on the side of a track, so I pulled out my poncho liner and wrapped it around Dan and he appeared to come right. He said that he was starting to feel warmer, so we continued toward the hut as I was concerned that we might now be caught in the open in a snowstorm.

About 500 metres from the hut Dan began to stagger and was on the verge of collapse. So I halted the stick and explained that the hut was only a few minutes walk. If we carried Dan, we could get him in a bed and shelter. Five of us carried Dan, and the sixth man, the corporal who had been map reading, ran on ahead to the hut, lit some candles and got the fire started. He took Dan's pack, and by the time we got there he had placed both sleeping bags one inside of the other on the largest bunk as I had instructed him in a previous lesson.

On arrival Dan was deeply unconscious, and we placed one of the ADGs into the sleeping bags and then the unconscious sergeant. I took out my survival blanket and tucked it over both men.

I then had the radio turned on, and as it was set on the unit's emergency frequency. I began transmitting, "Charlie Charlie One, this is Mike Sierra Five. No duff! Rifleman down, over!" (In New Zealand military jargon "No duff" informs all call signs on the net that your message is factual and not part of any exercise scenario.) There was no reply.

I tried several more times, on both our primary and secondary freqs, but there was no response. Due to our location and the height of the mountains, it was impossible to transmit to anywhere—we just had to tough it out. While serving with the New Zealand Air Force, I had seen many cases of hypothermia, both mild and serious, and so I knew that everything that the stick had done was correct and should save Sergeant Petty's life, it was just a matter of waiting. It was a long, long night.

At about 2300, he began stirring, and about 30 minutes later he regained consciousness. His first words in true Aussie fashion were, "Hey Kiwi, I could murder a beer mate."

The SOPs (Standard Operating Procedures) for hypothermia are very simple: no food or drink for several hours while the patient is monitored, and then sips of a warm, sweet liquid, usually tea. As well, once a member of a stick drops from hypothermia, no one moves from that loc-stat for a period of 24 hours as the actual patient, although he/she feels fine, is in a severely weakened state. I have even seen cases where a patient who is not monitored will go down for a second time, usually in a much more serious state.

The next morning I was outside the hut attempting to rig a long wire antennae when another instructor, Flight Lieutenant Ken Cunningham, moved through my loc with his own stick. When he asked why I wasn't moving, I explained about the problems we had encountered with Sergeant Petty and informed Ken that I did not intend to move until midday the following day. This did not please him as the entire squadron was required to be back at Woodbourne Airbase for a parade later that same day, and the drive from the training area took about two hours. When I gently reminded Ken about the SOPs and the sergeant's heart condition, he had to agree with me, and he then moved off with his stick. I was still fumbling with the long wire when in the far distance to the east came that very distinctive "waka! waka! waka!" of a Huey in flight. (In New Zealand, the jargon call sign for a Huey is "waka," which is also the Native New Zealand word for a war canoe.)

Hidden somewhere around my neck and under about four layers of clothing was my issue heliograph (a mirror with a hole in the centre and used for signaling). I scratched around for it and then moved to a flat clear area not far from the hut. The chopper was still a mere speck in the distance, and it was following the line of the river. It had just completed an NZSAS (New Zealand Special Air

Service) insertion. I put the heliograph to my right eye and then caught the sun's reflection. I dropped the reflection down at my feet, then moved it along the tussock and speargrass and then up to the index finger of my left hand, which I then aligned with the chopper. I began flashing, and then the da-da-da/dit-dit-dit/da-da-da of an SOS in Morse Code.

I had only just begun the second signal when the chopper banked slightly to the left and headed directly for me. I dropped the heliograph and yelled to the troopies beside me to saddle up and get Dan Petty ready for medevac on the now inbound chopper. I then stood with my back to the wind and raised my arms above my head in the classic V, "I am the Marshal," sign.

A few minutes later the chopper was overhead and flared above me, it was from 3 Squadron RNZAF. On landing I waited for the thumbs up and then ran toward the crewman. He removed his helmet and I was surprised to see that it was an old mate of mine, Barney Bevan, a Vietnam veteran who I had served with in 161 Battery. He was as surprised to see me as I was to see him. He put his helmet on and explained to the pilot about the sergeant's hypothermia and the need to get him back to Dip Flat Base Camp so that the medics could monitor his condition. The pilot then asked me how the rest of us were getting back. When I replied, "walking," he turned and grinned at me.

"Stuff walking, Mate, we'll fly you back," he said. Minutes later we were onboard the Huey and airborne—up over the beech trees and following the river down to the Rainbow Station road.

I received a commendation from my squadron leader for my actions during the incident, but I don't think that Ken Cunningham ever forgave me for taking the easy way out and flying home.

Postscript: Several weeks later I was called to my unit's office and was given a package by our chief clerk. When I opened it up, it was a hardcover book called *Henry Lawson's Images of Australia*. Henry Lawson was a famous Australian poet and it was widely known in the unit that I liked poetry. The inscription on the inside cover read as follows:

To:
Corporal Mike Subritzky
Senior GSI
RNZAF Woodbourne
From:
Sergeant Dan Petty
Fire Section
RAAF Garbutt

"In appreciation of assistance performed on the night of 17 June
1986 at Rainbow State Forest"
With thanks,
Dan Petty

✦ By Mike Subritzky
Senior GSI, Royal New Zealand Airforce

Read Mike Subritzky's poem "Air Assault" and his story "The Dear John" in
chapter 7.

📖

Winged Wisdom

ⓡ Never let anyone else navigate for you.
ⓡ If you are following someone, pay attention to the route anyway.

In the End, It Was Always the Hueys

This is not my story. This is the story of Galen Foster. It is the story of every
young boy who went to fight a war in a country called Vietnam. They went for
many reasons: some went to see the world, some went to better their chances in
life, some were drafted, and some enlisted. No matter what their reasons, they all
went with honor and for love of country. Many returned home old men a year
later, left to their silent selves to continue fighting the war in their minds; a war
which, for many, became forever emblazoned on their souls. This is also a story
about the Huey, the workhorse of Vietnam known to many as the "Angel of
Mercy." The Huey saved untold numbers of lives both during and after fierce
battles. ✦ Patty Biegun

Galen came from the sleepy town of Milstead, Georgia. He played football,
hung out at Beasley's Drug Store where he plunked down quarters for greasy
hamburgers, or, on a good night, took his date to Young and Ivey's for equally
greasy, yet more expensive, hamburgers and steaming bowls of heart-stopping
chili. He enjoyed working on hot rods and often cruised to Jack's in Decatur, a
20-minute drive from Milstead, in his freshly waxed 1937 Chevrolet Coupe.

Jack's was a favored hangout not for its burgers, fries, and shakes delivered to your car with a smile, but for shooting the bull, showing off cars, and meeting girls.

After graduation Galen took a job as a surveyor. When the work played out, he went to work for C&D Batteries in Conyers, Georgia, a stone's throw from Milstead.

Galen was a tall, striking boy with kind, lipid eyes, his face framed by thick, black, wavy hair that reminded one of a stormy sea on a moonless night. His nature, however, was anything but stormy. He was calm, reserved, and well-liked in his community. His family life was typical of rural America in the '60s. They lived in a modest house, went to church on Sundays, grew vegetables in their backyard, and had a black and white TV set. At a time when civil strife was coming to a head in larger cities and towns, Milstead, like many rural towns, seemed far removed from the evils of the world. In the evenings, when chores were done and dishes washed, Galen and his family sat in the safety of their living room watching the war play out on the nightly news. Bathed in a bluish glow radiating from the TV, they were ignorant of the fact that fate would soon rear its head and abruptly bring their "All American Life" to an end. Galen received his draft notice on March 22, 1966, five days after his 19th birthday.

By November of 1966, Galen had been "in country" for roughly a month and in the field for a week. He was the greenhorn, the FNG ("freaking" new guy), the guy who could save your life or get you killed. Galen demonstrated gallantry that seasoned units looked for in FNGs and was promptly embraced by the men of the 196th Light Infantry Brigade. They had confidence in Galen, the highest honor one soldier could bestow on another in a time of war. Within six weeks of his arrival in Vietnam, Galen would prove himself worthy of their trust.

It was a sizzling day as the 40 men of the 196th fought their way through the obdurate foliage of the flatlands of the Tay Ninh Province. Command had sent them out earlier in the week on a routine search and destroy mission: blowing a couple of tunnels and burning a few abandoned hooches where rice, suspect property of Charlie, had been stored. As far as war went, it had been an uneventful few days. Shortly before noon, as the sweltering heat intensified, the radioman signaled the CO (commanding officer). Another platoon had been pinned down and was taking heavy casualties. Galen's division was in close proximity; they were instructed to immediately change course. The 196th had been handed an invitation to hell, and there was no RSVP.

Already entangled in vines that wrapped around seemingly impenetrable foliage and towering trees that wiped out the sun, they dug deeper into the jungle, becoming more bunched up as they cursed and fought the terrain. Several soldiers had to walk point as one man slung his machete, cutting a swathe through the denseness of the bamboo and undergrowth. The machete made sharp swooshing noises that could have easily echoed their position to the waiting enemy. The point men were on high alert.

As the men slowly fought their way through the jungle, the sounds of gunfire and explosions became closer. Adrenaline was flowing; sweat streamed from every pore, making irregular patterns in dirt-encrusted faces. Mosquitoes dined on muscular flesh as helmets bobbed up and down; weapons, M-14s, M-79s, M-16s, M-60s, .45 caliber pistols, grenades, and knives, reverberated against bodies as the jungle slowly corralled the 196th into one mass unit moving at a snail's pace toward an appointment with destiny. With each step Galen tightened his grip on his M-79 grenade launcher. Before that fateful day, the worse thing that had happened to Galen was the occasional whizzing of a bullet by his head, courtesy of a sniper. Premonitions told Galen and the rest of the 196th there would be no casual sniper fire on this day. They were poised for the worst. They would not be disappointed.

Soldiers had a saying, "Charlie knows when you are coming." He was alert, silent, invisible, patient, and struck when it was least expected. They were waiting for the 196th on that fateful day in November, and hit them with mighty force at a time of their choosing. Simultaneously, the enemy began firing as soldiers were confronted by either surface mines or trip wires. Several men went down. It was chaos as Galen heard several more explosions, one knocking him to the ground. Covered with blood, and accepting he had been hit, he grabbed his M-79 and went back into action. His men needed him—as long as he could stand he would fight. After the initial shock, he saw the body of a faceless soldier who had seconds before been standing in front of him. Galen had not been hit. It was his buddy's blood that stained his clothes and ran down his face.

An eternity had passed in a split second; incoming fire seemed to be coming from all directions. Their platoon leader had been killed and, stunned by the initial blasts, the unit was momentarily disoriented. The platoon sergeant took command; getting the sighting he needed, he pointed straight ahead. The 196th let loose with all they had; weapons fired in unison, their bullets and rockets combining to make thunderous noises as they screeched through the air. Galen dropped to the ground and crawled over bodies trying to get to his left where a semblance of a clearing would give him a better advantage in delivering devastating blows to the enemy. An exploding 79 near his men was not an option. As Galen began his assault on Charlie, voices pitched and fell in the air. The deafening explosions did little to buffer neither the cursing of the soldiers as M-16s jammed nor the cries of agony as wounded soldiers screamed for the medic. Dodging bullets, their medic rushed from body to body, passing the dead by, doing what he could for those who needed immediate attention and moving back to those with lesser injuries. He could have used another hand on that day.

As the battle intensified, the sergeant called in coordinates for artillery fire. He began yelling over the radio as men fell to friendly fire in the tight theatre that left no margin for error. The battlefield was becoming littered with blood and bodies, ripped trees, empty casings, and discarded medical paraphernalia. The nauseating mixture of the smells of blood and gunpowder stagnated in the air. Galen kept popping 79s into the now thinning jungle as he and others scrambled to get a better position on the enemy. The minutes ticked by like days, but no one was thinking about time now. Suddenly there was silence. It was over in an hour.

There was no time to delay. The whop-whop of the Hueys could be heard in the distance. Both units knew Charlie could have called for support or be regrouping for another assault. Some soldiers tried to get a quick body count on Charlie as their wounded comrades were rushed to the waiting Dustoffs. As usual, the enemy had retreated, taking most of his wounded and dead with him. Getting to the Hueys swiftly was paramount. Eventually both units safely worked their way to the clearing, some carrying the dead and wounded, some helping to hold up those who could still walk. The sight of six Hueys waiting in the clearing looked like a mirage that might at any moment disappear. They hurried the wounded aboard and nervously awaited the arrival of more Hueys. Some 80 or so men had to be swiftly evacuated.

The waiting men watched for Charlie and listened intently for the sound of the incoming Hueys. One by one, Hueys materialized in groups over the horizon. The heat rising from the blistering earth made them look like distorted green angels in the distance. As the Hueys approached, gunners could be seen hanging from skids as they kept a sharp lookout for signs of the enemy. Grasses parted, bent, and swirled around the waiting men as the Hueys neared and lowered, their skids dropping with mighty thuds; one Huey, two Hueys, three Hueys, followed by others. The men shielded their eyes against the dust, ducked their heads, and darted toward the Angel of Mercy as the forceful wind pushed against their drained bodies.

Looking like old men, the soldiers climbed aboard and held on as the Huey pilots pulled pitch, leaving a swirl of debris behind them. The wind felt good against their scorched faces. Most of the men said nothing. Like Galen, they only peered down at the surrealistic landscape below them, the grass still struggling against the downwind from the Huey's blades. As Galen's Huey rose above the trees and headed for base, he looked back at the battlefield where he had aged a million years. He thought only of those who were lost and wounded and of the Hueys. They had all fought bravely for each other, but, in the end, it was always the Hueys and their brave crews who came to take them out of hell.

Back at base camp, Galen and his men washed off the blood and dirt, talked little, and waited. In a few days replacements would be sent in and the 196th would be handed another mission. It would be Galen's turn to size up the FNGs.

✦ By Patty Biegun
http://www.aurence.net
http://www.aurence.net/photog.htm

Galen Foster returned to Milstead in September of 1967, where he went back to work for C&S Technologies and literally married the girl next door. Galen and his wife have one child and two grandchildren. Galen is still employed for C&S Technology, now C&D Batteries. For 36 years Galen Foster never spoke of Vietnam. In telling his story now he has begun the process of healing, and he hopes it will help others to understand the need to talk with their loved ones about their experiences in Vietnam. He says he is no hero. He was doing his job. To Galen, the heroes are the men who fought beside him and those who shed their blood in the Tay Ninh Province. And, of course, the Huey crews who shuttled the wounded to safety and picked up his remaining men. Ask him if he would do it again, and he says, "I love this great country in which we live. If they needed me to fight again, I would be proud to do so." This writer believes him.

Galen served with the 196th Light Infantry Brigade, 2nd Battalion, 1st Infantry, 2nd Platoon, 2nd Squad. He apologies if his memory was a little foggy. After all, for 36 years he has tried to forget. ✦ Patty Biegun

Read Patty Biegun's wedding story, "A Huey Tail Come True," chapter 11.

CHAPTER 9

Bullets With No Names

To fly as fast as thought,
you must begin by knowing
that you have already arrived.

Richard Bach, 1936–present
Jonathan Livingston Seagull

God's Fingerprint

In 1969, I was flying Dustoff from a "standby" position between Da Nang and Chu Lai. An evacuation mission was called in for us to fly out and pick up a wounded enemy soldier and transport him to an aid station. The area was not a "hot" area for enemy activity, and therefore the mission seemed routine.

As I turned low and fast into the smoke that marked the pickup position, a Viet Cong soldier flipped open the cover of his "spider hole" and emptied the magazine of an AK-47 toward my ship. I heard, through my earphones and over the sound of the engine, that unmistakable sound of bullets passing through my aircraft.

We flew the ship directly to a maintenance facility where we inspected the damage. I saw where one of the bullets had entered the bottom of the aircraft below where I had been sitting. I went inside the ship to find where the bullet had come up through the floor and how close I had come to being hit. I could find no hole.

Just that morning, I had placed a metal ammo box of M-16 cartridges on the floor beside my seat. Dustoff ships were allowed to carry small arms to protect their patients. When I turned the ammo box upside down, I saw where the bullet had entered but not exited the box of ammo, nor had the ammo exploded.

Aligning the holes in the ship, the path of the bullet was such that it would have entered my chest just below my right rib cage and exited somewhere near my left shoulder. Opening the box of ammo, I retrieved what was left of the spent round. It still had my name on it.

A bullet knows no premeditation and has no conscience. It is obedient only to the laws of physics, Sir Isaac Newton, and God.

There are those who believe in fate, predestination, and divine intervention. There are those who do not. I am not sure where my beliefs fit into that equation. Perhaps there are some inevitable cosmic projectiles for each of us—orbiting and taking aim out there in space somewhere, and having our names on them. Perhaps we delay that meeting by setting an ammo box beside our seat, placing a book on a table, leaving two minutes late in the morning, or pausing to offer a kindness. I simply do not know.

I still wonder at the events of 30 years ago and how and why an ammo box was there to stop a bullet with my name on it. In the ignorance and arrogance of my youth, I probably found some way to take credit for my own salvation. I search now for a truth, and wish that I had looked more closely and more gently at that fragmented chunk of lead—to have found not only my name but perhaps, some single, fragile fingerprint of God.

✦ By Bob Mackey
Dustoff pilot, RVN 1969–1970

Read Bob Mackey's comments on "Everyone's A Hero," chapter 4.
Note: A "spider hole" is a small hole dug into the earth with a thatched lid placed on top to conceal the enemy soldier inside. This name may have been given because of its similarity to the hunting methods of the trapdoor spider.
✦ Bob Mackey

📖

Winged Wisdom

જ Look people in the eye when you give them a safety briefing.
જ Smile at your passengers—it makes them relax.
જ If you feel woozy, check your altitude.

Donut Dollies

Jim, my door gunner, and I got up early, grabbed some chow at the mess hall, and just took a minute to enjoy the peace and quiet of the early morning. After breakfast we went to our hooch to retrieve our weapons. We each carried a .45 caliber sidearm, an M-16, and a sweet firing M-60 fully automatic machine gun.

My pilots were Bullet and Mr. Tibbs, and the four of us were scheduled for standby this day. What that means is we were available for anything a Huey can handle. It could be a medical run, aircraft recovery, combat assault, or nothing at all. We got the helicopter ready to go and just hung around. It looked like it might be a good day of much needed rest.

About 1100 hours we flew a few sorties. The first one was to fly to Saigon, pick up about nine Donut Dollies, and fly them to a firebase so they could entertain the troops. We would drop them at the firebase and fly a couple of resupply sorties, return and pick up the girls, and on back to Saigon. Very easy day all in all.

Got my Huey checked out, guns were cleaned and lubed, and grenades secured. The pilots did their preflight, and we lit the fire to this jet fuel-drinking flying machine. All systems were a go, and I heard the pilot say, "Satellite 318, west revetment, request taxi to active for a south departure." The tower gave us clearance and we pulled up to a hover, performed our power checks, and were on our way. As we cleared the safety of our compound, the pilot, as always, gave us the command to "Lock and load, test fire your weapons on your command." No problem, I love to fire a belt-fed machine from my helicopter. There was just something about the noise, smell, shaking, and the empty brass pinging off the floor. The gunner and I let go 100 rounds or so and just watched the bullets ripple in the rice paddy below.

With that out of the way, we quickly gained altitude to get out of .30 caliber range, and headed to Saigon. With Saigon only 15 minutes away, we could relax, take in the view, and have a smoke. Watching the sun come up in Vietnam at altitude is one of my fondest memories of being there. The smell and the warm blast of air hitting me in the face were most calming. Too bad that calm could not last all day every day.

Got clearance to land at pad Hotel #3, and as we were coming in we could see the American women. A nice sight for young, lonely helicopter warriors. We landed, got the pretty ladies strapped in. God, my helicopter smelled good! I had to keep my dark tinted visor down so they could not see me staring. They were all smiles and excited. Just doing their naïve thing for God and Country like the rest of us. Yes, we would take very good care of our special cargo this morning.

We lifted off gently and flew to an armor firebase not far from the border. I always thought this was a little risky for noncombatants, but what do I know? Anyway, we found the firebase; all the armor vehicles were pulled into a circle for security like wagon trains from the Old West. We landed in the middle and helped the ladies off.

As we took off, the ladies were setting up their gig. The guys, of course, were hovering around them. There are no words to describe what it was like to see some American women in the middle of this lonely, scary war. It was a breath of fresh air, and this would be a nice distraction for the soldiers for sure.

We had a few sorties to fly the rest of the day and would return later to pick up the girls. We would be thinking about that ride the rest of the day. We were gone less than an hour when we received an urgent radio call: "Satellite 318, return immediately to Firebase XYZ, we are taking fire."

Well, here we go, now we can show our stuff and rescue the "damsels in distress." We maxed out our airspeed and got on the deck. As we approached the firebase we could see the tracks firing their big guns; hell, everyone was firing. We radioed them and told them we were going to do a low, high-speed approach, and we were going to fly right over the bad guys to show them what kind of force we had. Then, if needed we could call in the fast boys with napalm. We did our fast approach while the gunner and I just kept blasting away.

We saw no enemy, they would have been foolish to poke their heads up. We flared hard, the Huey bucking and groaning as we stressed every rivet in it. The pilot brought the bird to a classic "Hot LZ" landing. The gunner and I jumped out, told the girls to leave their equipment and get on now. Those poor girls were terrified—crying and in shock. We picked up a couple and threw them in the helicopter. They did not mind. I think they knew what a target we were sitting on the ground.

I put one woman in the gun well with me, and we did a max performance takeoff. I was holding this pretty lady's head down with one hand and blasting away with my other. Hot brass was bouncing off her as I was doing my best to put 600 rounds per minute out of my machine gun. The noise was, I am sure, just awful for them, deafening in fact. It did nothing to calm them down. We climbed as fast and as high as possible to get out of .30 caliber range. Once we achieved that, we leveled off and checked the girls out for any injuries. There were no physical ones.

They started to collect themselves after a while. I let my lady's head up, got some of the brass out of her hair, and gave her a hug while telling her, "It's all over and you're safe."

She tried a weak smile and thanked me.

"No, thank you," I told her, "for you to risk your lives for little pay just to put a smile on our faces is most admirable."

We were heroes that day for them, and we loved and hammed up every minute of it. The pilots were jealous for sure.

Not a bad day all in all. When people say negative things about the Red Cross, I always remember that day. These women were not the managers or corporate folks. They were "the girl next door," and they risked their lives for me and thousands of others. It was my job to risk my life for them, but they did not have to come to Nam much less to an unsecured firebase. Some of them died in Vietnam, and I am very sorry I couldn't have been there for them. For that, I salute you, Donut Dollies, may God Bless you.

Just another day in "The Nam" and in a soldier's story.

✦ By Larry Harty
Master Sergeant (retired), 2nd Signal Group, 1st Signal Brigade, RVN 1970–1971

Read more adventures of the crew of Satellite 318 in Harty's story in this book, "Trick or Treat," chapter 5. Read more stories by and about the American Red Cross Donut Dollies in the Vietnam War in *Angels in Vietnam: Women Who Served.*

📖

Flight Facts: Male soldiers weren't the only ones who used helicopters for transportation in the Vietnam War. From 1962 to 1974, the United States sent paid volunteers from the American Red Cross to assist the military personnel in Vietnam. The young women of the American Red Cross were divided into three groups: the SMH (Service to Military Hospitals) served in the hospitals and provided social work and recreational therapy for the injured and rehabilitating patients; the SMI (Service to Military Installations) arranged compassionate emergency leave for soldiers, and they passed on information to the soldiers from home in regard to emergencies, births, and deaths; and the SRAO (Supplemental Recreational Activities Overseas) or Donut Dollies as they had been nicknamed in World War II, brought games and conversation to the soldiers in the field. They also ran recreation centers for the enlisted men. They offered smiles, games, and a break from the war for the military personnel. The Donut Dollies traveled by jeep and helicopter to reach the thousands of soldiers at military command posts as well as remote field sites. ✦ Information courtesy of Sharon Vander Ven

Cummings, American Red Cross SRAO "Donut Dolly," April 1966–April 1967, www.illyria.com/rccummings.html. Condensed and reprinted here from *Angels in Vietnam: Women Who Served.*

CHAPTER 10

Chasing Rainbows

Man's dream of flying is an unfinished saga,
carrying us now toward even greater adventures in outer space.
But wherever we may go, and whatever we achieve
through our efforts to push back the horizon of our knowledge,
Igor Sikorsky will remain a source of inspiration
—a true man of vision.

Richard Nixon, 1913–1994

Winged Wisdom

୧ Go on a helicopter flight at least once in your life.
୧ When life goes awry, remember that once upon a time
you flew high above the trees, with the eagles, into the clouds.
୧ Don't fly into the trees on purpose.
୧ Don't fly into a flock of birds on purpose.
୧ Don't fly into the clouds on purpose.

The Perfect Day

I spent 20 years in the United States Air Force, and in those 20 years I had the opportunity to fly on helicopters about three or four times. I flew in England as well as Japan, but none was more enjoyable than the 30-minute ride my family and I took with Blue Hawaiian Helicopters on a summer vacation in Maui.

The trip was not cheap, but my wife and I both made up our minds that this was the chance of a lifetime, and we didn't know if we'd ever get back to such a tropical paradise. So, we decided to go for it. Our children, Jackie and Jennifer, were as excited as we were.

Our pilot was Steve Schaefer, an ordained minister who flew for Blue Hawaiian on the side. We couldn't have asked for a more professional and friendly pilot to be our tour guide.

After a short video on the safety features of our aircraft, we were strapped in by the friendly staff of Blue Hawaiian. The weather was absolutely perfect. Temperatures were in the high 70s with the sun shining brightly. Steve played Elvis Presley's "Stuck on You" to put us in the mood. Flying over the city of Kahalui, we came across fields of macadamia nuts as well as acres and acres of sugar cane. Since 70 percent of the island of Maui can only be seen by helicopter, we were in for a real treat.

Flying over the mountain peaks, green valleys, and gorges where the films *Lilo and Stitch* and *Jurrasic Park* were inspired, it was beauty to behold. The water was as blue as blue can be. We flew over the coast of Lahina where numerous para-sailers were having a wonderful time.

The highlight for me was seeing both ends of a gorgeous rainbow up close and personal. Also, watching the white fluffy clouds and feeling like you could just walk over them was exactly what one might picture heaven to be like. The only things missing were the angels.

The half-hour helicopter ride was truly the highlight of our week in Maui.

I've been to 15 countries and more than 40 states in my lifetime, but our helicopter ride convinced me that God made Maui one of the most special and beautiful places on earth.

✝ By Ken Melusky

Winged Wisdom

ᴄᴚ Always have a flight plan.
ᴄᴚ Always carry a map.
ᴄᴚ Make sure your maps are current.
ᴄᴚ Always study the map before taking off.
ᴄᴚ Never trust a cow as a navigational aid.

Living the Dream

The official document read, "You have been ordered to attend the Rotary Wing Officer Basic Course at Ft. Rucker, AL," or something very close to that anyway.

It was a feeling that is almost impossible to put into words. For those of you who have received a similar letter, you know that feeling. I may have even been a little more excited to receive that letter than most because of my age at the time. As I recall, the Army said that you could not be more than 26 ½ years old at application, or 27 ½ years old at graduation from flight training. I was 29 when I received the letter and 30 ½ years old when I graduated.

For once in my life my timing was right. It was 1979, and the Indiana National Guard had not received training money or flight school "slots" for several years. The end of the Viet Nam war had allowed pilots leaving active duty to continue their flying careers in Guard units across the country. This pool of trained pilots coming off of active duty tours had finally started drying up, and the Guard bureau had not allocated training money to bridge the gap. My Guard unit was really hurting for junior commissioned officers to fill platoon leader positions. Because they had turned so many eager applicants away for so many years, no one was asking in 1979—except me!

I was a "crusty" old first lieutenant with ten years enlisted time, who had just recently discovered that the aviation battalion needed commissioned pilots. Since I was the only one around and they had new training money, I requested an age waver and it was granted.

I reported to Ft. Rucker in March of 1979. About 25% of my classmates were West Point graduates, and all the rest were active duty officers. I was the only National Guardsman in the class. It didn't take long to understand where I was on the pecking order as the sole "National Guard guy." I felt from day one that I had something to prove to the rest of the class, especially the "ring knockers."

A class of around 35 to 40 students started new training cycles about once a month. Each class was distinguished from the other classes by a different colored baseball cap. After a few weeks you knew which colored hat was in what phase of training. This way, you knew when to feel superior or subordinate based on the color of a hat! As luck would have it, I was a Brown hat. Not the coolest color to be worn with my new one piece Nomex flight suit, but I was just happy to be at the home of Army Aviation, living out a dream.

The next distinguishing marking was a pair of fabric wings with an "S" on the center emblem, sewn on the front of the colored cap. These wings indicated that you had, in fact, successfully taken off and returned to earth alone and unassisted.

The "S" on the wings stood for "solo." There was much awe and respect for the students who wore solo wings on their hats. I'm pretty certain that everyone wanted to be the first in class to be awarded the coveted solo wings. As luck would have it, I was the first in my class to solo. I promptly ran to the PX (Post Exchange), purchased my fabric wings, had them sewn on my hat at the tailor shop, and was wearing them the next morning in class. What a fantastic feeling that was. Not only was I the "National Guard guy," but I was also the oldest guy in class. My status quietly changed, at least in my mind. What my classmates never knew was what happened on my first solo cross-country flight.

The first aircraft we learned to fly was the Hughes TH-55. It was a small two-seater with a bubble windshield and a piston engine. It was a pretty basic helicopter, but extremely fun to fly. Because there were so many flight students in the air at any given time, each class was assigned to a stagefield for their training flights. The aircraft were based at one of several large heliports at Ft. Rucker, and we flew from there to one of the many smaller stagefields constructed all over southern Alabama.

In this first phase of flight training, my class was assigned to a stagefield about eight miles southeast of the heliport. The TH-55s were assigned to Hanchey Army Heliport where they shared half of the very large ramp with a CH-47 Chinook unit. On one side of the ramp were these little orange bubble-nosed trainers, and on the other side were the giant OD (olive-drab) green, twin-rotor Chinooks. We were in awe of these massive giants and could not yet imagine that some of us might one day be flying them.

Two students were paired up with an instructor pilot and one TH-55. One student flew the first period with the instructor while the other one rode an Army bus out to the stagefield. The first student and instructor finished their flight at the stagefield and debriefed. The second student and instructor returned the air-craft to the main heliport while the first student rode the bus back. Very efficient. I had flown the route from the main heliport to the stagefield with my instructor several times before my instructor announced that I would fly the first period alone. I was so pumped up with adrenaline that by the time I pulled pitch I hardly knew my name.

I departed Hanchey AHP (Army Heliport) with the blessing of the tower controller and began my journey to Toth stagefield. I climbed to my assigned en route altitude of about 1,500 feet and proceeded to my corridor entry point. I entered the corridor so full of myself and the dream of solo flight that I completely forgot to watch the route and identify the checkpoint for the first turn toward the stagefield. When my brain finally kicked in, I was somewhere over southern Alabama that was totally unfamiliar to me. I'd never flown anywhere other than that training corridor and the stagefield traffic pattern. Mild panic began to set in. I had not been trained on map navigation yet, and I certainly could not do that and fly this aircraft at the same time! I was not concerned about my safety because I was confident that I could get the aircraft back on the ground without incident. I was, although, very concerned that I was going to be the subject of a search and rescue, which would surely end my very short flying career.

Vanity and ego quickly set in, and I was determined that I could solve this dilemma before anyone was the wiser. I remembered that we turned east to the stagefield, so I turned east hoping to spot it off in the distance. I flew for about five minutes and did not see anything recognizable. Unsure of what to do, I continued flying east, deducing that I had just not gone far enough yet.

Suddenly I noticed several large and small aircraft at varying altitudes all around me. A more thorough search of the landscape revealed a large metropolitan airport that was totally unfamiliar to me. My radio was still tuned to one of the two frequencies that I needed for this training flight and not to the airport's tower. I was sure that this airport control tower was trying desperately to reach me on their frequency to alert me that I was an accident looking for a place to happen. I decided to exit the airspace as quickly as possible before anyone noticed the bright orange helicopter.

I now figured that west was my best bet, so I did a quick 180 and headed back from where I came. I tried to calm myself down, while at the same time envisioning my instructor pilot telling me to pack my bags and head for Indiana. After several minutes I decided to turn back north because I had no doubt gone too far south. I flew north for about 10 minutes, searching desperately for something on the ground that looked familiar. I was beside myself with panic when something occurred to me—the higher you are above the earth, the farther you can see! I convinced myself that if I continued heading north and climbing, I would have a better-than-average chance of spotting Hanchey with all of those great big Chinooks!

I began a climb to somewhere between three and four thousand feet. This in itself was semi-traumatic because I had never been alone in a small helicopter with the doors off above 1,500 feet. Looking out on the horizon, I did see a string of Chinooks and followed my gaze along the string backwards. Low and behold, there was Hanchey! Just about that time I realized that the Hanchey tower controller was attempting to contact the TH-55 inbound to Hanchey from the south.

"Identify yourself," he repeated several times. What do I do now I asked myself—answer the controller and tell him I'm a lost student who is wandering around Southern Alabama looking for something recognizable? After all, that would be the correct thing to do. Placing correctness aside, I decided that risking my very short Army Aviation career was not an option at this time. I quickly focused on the Heliport and spotted the takeoff pad where I first began this journey. I did a quick descending 180 turn to get back on the original departure corridor at the proper altitude. Paying extremely close attention to the route, I spotted the checkpoint where I was supposed to turn east the first time. I made the turn and started picking up all of the landmarks that would lead me to the stagefield where I was supposed to be doing traffic pattern work. Toth stagefield began to come into view on the horizon where multiple TH-55s were doing takeoffs and landings.

I changed my radio to the stagefield frequency and maneuvered myself into position to join the traffic pattern at the standard 45-degree entry. I made the radio call to enter traffic on the downwind leg and slipped into line. I looked at my watch and realized that my hour was about up, and it was time for me to land and shut down for student change.

My heart started racing as I realized how much trouble I might really be in. The stagefield controller or my instructor had no doubt realized that I had not arrived when I was supposed to, and there was now a full-scale search and rescue effort underway. Or, Dothan Metropolitan Airport had reported that wayward orange helicopter to the Hanchey control tower who in turn reported to the Toth tower that they must have a missing student!

I landed and hovered into the first available pad. I set the aircraft down and shut it down by the checklist. I completed my logbook entries, watched as the refueler topped off the tanks, and headed for the building where my instructor and all my classmates were surely waiting for my arrival with a mixture of snickers and grins. I opened the screen door and stepped inside. I spotted my instructor sitting at a table with my stick-buddy filling out a flight plan.

He looked up at me and said in his professional instructor voice, "How did everything go?"

I starred at him for about five seconds and answered "Great!"

He shook my hand and said he would see me back at Hanchey for the debriefing. I knew now that I had successfully pulled off a completely boneheaded flight and broken numerous flight and training rules along the way. I was the first to solo and the first to fly solo to a stagefield. Most everyone on the bus was surely envious of me. How ironic. I don't know which emotion was strongest on that long, hot July bus ride back to Hanchey AHP: pride, humility, shame, or fear.

I learned several lessons that day, which helped me stay much more focused for the remainder of my flight training and aviation career. I experienced what would later become known as "task overload." Task overload is a relative condition that can manifest itself very early in the life of a young, overconfident student pilot. I chose not to share my experience with my instructor pilot at the debriefing. I decided to spare him the anguish of humiliation for sending me on a solo flight before I was really ready. Yeah, right. I did go to the Officers' Club that night to have a beer and celebrate the fact that I had survived a very sloppy solo flight and the fact that I was still living my dream.

✦ By James M. Dunbar
   CW4, Army retired, 1980–2000, Master Aviator

Read James Dunbar's story "A Failure to Communicate," chapter 1.

📖

Flight Facts: The U. S. Army acquired its first helicopter in 1947. Camp (Fort) Sill, Oklahoma, became the Army Aviation School in 1953. Until then, the Air Force provided primary training for Army Aviation pilots.

Two years prior to Bell's introduction of the Huey, in 1954, the Army moved its aviation school to Camp (Fort) Rucker, Alabama, where the Army still trains its pilots today. Until 1973, however, pilots did their primary training at Fort Wolters, Texas, then went to Fort Rucker for the next phase of training. During the Vietnam War, many pilots also received training at Hunter Army Airfield/Fort Stewart, Georgia. In 1973, pilots began doing all of their training at Fort Rucker. Aviation became its own branch in the Army in 1983.

In helicopter flight school, students who fly in the same helicopter refer to one another as stick buddies. Stick is the term for the cyclic control.

Winged Wisdom

ଔ Encourage others to follow their dreams.
ଔ Never give up on your own dreams.
ଔ Inner beauty lasts.

The Right Stuff

"You will not, under any circumstances, for any reason, get on any helicopter at any time, your entire year here." Those were the only words I remember my Chief Nurse saying at my in processing. It was just before Thanksgiving, 1970, in Cam Ranh Bay, Vietnam.

On Christmas Eve, with a set of bogus orders in my hand, I boarded a Huey bound for Nha Trang. Apparently all the nurse fatalities, save one who died from an enemy attack, had occurred in helicopter or plane crashes so far in this war.

As we lifted off the helipad I felt the familiar rush of what it feels like when you can actually fly in your dreams. I felt that lightness and unreal sensation of whisking around in the skies, untouchable, inviolate, away from the perils that lurk on the earth.

We banked out over the South China Sea and I saw my compound from the air get smaller, and the stress of caring for the wounded was replaced with the wonderful adrenaline rush I was beginning to crave more and more with each day in country.

A couple of the doctors had arranged for us to be "disinterested parties" to check narcotics at the dispensary, and I was happy to go along with the charade. I can't recall seeing the dispensary, but the flight was worth the risk. What were they going to do, send me to Vietnam?

We had lunch at a beautiful little seaside restaurant called "Francois." Francois himself greeted us, showed us to our table, brought us French wine, and we ordered the lobster salad. He brought out three live lobsters on a platter and one was chosen to be our lunch.

I'd never had lobster before, but that was just one of the incredible, sensual experiences of the day. After lunch, as we were stepping across the dirt road to get in the jeep, one of the docs put his arm in front of me as our driver trotted over to check the jeep for booby traps. Oh yeah, I forgot, we were in a war zone. Determining all was well, we piled into the jeep and were off to our stallion of the skies. Our pilot was a crusty old second-tour warrant officer. He was delighted to have a nurse to show off for.

"Happy to take you for a ride, LT, you won't get sick on me will you?" he said with a mischievous grin.

"Nothing you can do will make me sick, Chief!" It was a challenge.

We flew like the wind, doing NOE (nap of the earth), just barely clearing the treetops, up and over the hills, down into the valleys; better than any ride at Disneyland. We were strapped in, but the lovely thing about the choppers in Nam is there were no doors. You could feel the wind, the changes in humidity; smell all the different aromas of the land, the people, and the sea. It was a day of experiencing all the senses so acutely. I felt so alive, and my skin tingled as my innards rose and fell with the pitching of this magnificent machine in the hands of this expert.

When I started to turn a slight shade of green, I guess he figured I'd had enough, and he probably didn't relish cleaning lobster off the deck of his Huey, so we changed pace. We flew out to a firebase and I waved to the troops on the ground; they came streaming out of tents and bunkers like ants as the word spread there was a blonde overhead. We flew by a giant Buddha statue, which I had the presence of mind to photograph. The tour was over all too soon and our beautiful bird dropped us back at our hospital.

Nothing was ever said about it, I'd gotten away with it. I was invincible! But then we all felt that way at 21. With all of the horrible things that happened in that year that I have repressed, that one day was one I have remembered in detail all these years. To be free from the earth, to hover like a bee, and dive like an eagle, safe in the hands of one who knows his stuff. Now that's living.

✛ By Janis Nark

Janis Nark, Lt. Col., USAR (Retired), served for 26 years in the Army Nurse Corps with assignments that included Vietnam and Desert Storm. She has lived on three different continents, made a point of going where no women were invited, and now lives to tell about it. She is a highly sought after motivational speaker who addresses the areas of change and stress with content, humor, and scalpel-sharp insights for succeeding in today's chaotic world.

She is a published author whose stories are currently in nine popular books including *A 4th Course of Chicken Soup for the Soul, Chicken Soup for the Nurse's Soul, Why Vietnam Still Matters*, and *Angels In Vietnam: Women Who Served*. She has many of her speeches available on CD and audio tape, including "Celebrating Our Strengths: The 10 Things Powerful Women Do" and "A Woman Looks Back at War." To find out more about Janis Nark, to purchase books or tapes, or to book her for a speaking engagement: JanisNark@aol.com, www.nark.com, or 828-652-5490.

CHAPTER 11

Broken Dreams, Mended Hearts

*I was annoyed from the start by the attitude of doubt by the spectators
that I would never really make the flight.
This attitude made me more determined than ever to succeed.*

Harriet Quimby, 1875-1912
America's first licensed female pilot

Winged Wisdom

ob Make time for your family.
ob Judge your success on your happiness not on your income.

A Huey Tail Come True

I must be the only helicopter in history to have been cast in a real-life fairy tale. My name is 091, or at least that's what they call me. They call me other names, too: "Angel of Mercy" and "Huey," to name a few. Actually, I am a Bell UH-1H Iroquois helicopter, but I was never impressed by that name. I like 091. It's a nickname taken from my tail number, 65-10091. I am a veteran of the Vietnam War. Through monsoons, dusty hot days, and coal-black nights, I was a loyal workhorse for those who depended on me, namely the *Robin Hoods*, a brave bunch of soldiers, officially the 173rd Assault Helicopter Company. I was shot up twice and eventually moved out of Vietnam where I went from home to home: the National Guard, Army Flight Training School, NASA, and places in between.

112

In 1995, someone deemed me too old, I guess, and I was retired to the Texas Air Command Museum. At first, it was nice to take a rest, but after awhile I became bored and sat around reminiscing about the old days—pulling pitch in clouds of smoke as bullets screamed around my thin skin, sometimes piercing my sides with pings that echoed for miles over the treetops, dropping into hot LZs surrounded by VC and flying soldiers to safety. Sighing, I thought, "If I could only fly one more time."

The old UH-I Fairy Godmother in the Sky must have heard my prayers. In 2002, news began to circulate that I had been leased to a production company. They were going to fly me around the country on a healing mission. My motor was pumping as things started to spin and it wasn't my tired old blades. I was soon carted off for a complete rehaul and paint job, complete with *Robin Hood* nose art. I had been reborn and I was ready to serve my men again. I thought I was dreaming until on October 2, 2002, amidst great fanfare and looking like the day I was born, I lifted off from Fort Rucker in Alabama.

From Fort Rucker to Angel Fire, New Mexico, I flew 10,000 miles, meeting the valiant men and women who served in Vietnam, as well as their families and friends. People crawled all over me; they laughed, cried, rode in me, touched me, but most importantly we were instantly connected in the spirit of brotherhood and sisterhood. Everywhere I went, long before they heard the whop–whop from my spinning blades, something extraordinary happened. We all came together on a mission of peace, a mission of remembrance, and a mission that would forever honor all those who fought and died in Vietnam. The people I met became my family; their tears became the blood we shared on the battlefield so many years ago. Every place I landed was a unique experience, but there was one place that I hold dear to my heart—Demorest, Georgia.

The backyard of Larry and Patty Hancock, aka Aurence and Biegun, instantly reminded me of Vietnam. When I topped the trees, I saw the flare signaling my LZ pointed to a tiny spot surrounded by hills and more trees. A muddy river banked by oaks, poplars, and high weeds ran to the right of where I was to land; to the left I would have to fight blueberry bushes and to the front of my cockpit, more poplars. If I lost wind on my descent, my tail could easily hit the blueberries or tall weeds and put me into a spin. If my 48-foot diameter rotor blades went a few feet in the wrong direction, I would hit the poplars and oaks. There was no margin for error in any direction. It had to be a perfect landing. I had to be *The Little Huey That Could*. "Hell," I thought, "this is a football field compared to some of the LZs from some 30 years ago." I was old but I still had guts. Not to be bragging, but after about 20 minutes of circles, dropping, and pulling pitch, I landed like an angel on a downy cloud. I'm sure the waiting crowd saw a glimmer of a smile as my skids touched the cooling October earth.

My excitement over, I was greeted by waiting veterans and Aurence and Biegun, both full of tears, something I had become accustomed to on my journey. Aurence had been a door gunner on the UH-34, CH-37, and of course, on one of my relatives; the latter, I'm sure, he holds in higher regard. As with all of my landings, stories were told, moments of life and death relived, and speeches made. The air thick with emotions made this old tin can want to cry jet fuel.

As the afternoon waned, the skies, which had earlier threatened rain, began to open up and the whole earth was bathed in a golden sunset reminiscent of so many I had seen in Vietnam. Take away the war, and the country was a beautiful place. Just when I thought the day could not get any better, people began to gather around me and light candles and incense. A young girl began to play a haunting melody on her flute as Aurence, dressed in fatigues, wearing a ragged Purple Heart (I heard him say he had received it at the hospital in Da Nang), and Rev. Bill McDonald, dressed in his flight suit and collar, joined each other on my starboard side. I saw Biegun appearing from the road that wound up the shadowy hill and into the dense trees that hid their house. She was wearing an ao dai, a Vietnamese wedding dress. It was bright red with soft clouds of white that looked as if they had fallen from the sky and landed there; its gold glitter sparkled in the setting sun. On her head she wore a matching ao dai hat. Gracefully, she glided down to us and took her place by Aurence, her husband of 25 years. Each holding a single white rose, they recited vows each had written. Aurence pledged his undying love and Biegun made us all cry with her words:

"Twenty-five years ago, I married Larry Aurence Hancock. Today, I will marry one of "The Few. The Proud"—a United States Marine. I will marry a Vietnam veteran. I will marry my best friend. Today by this Huey, I once again commit myself to my hero, Larry Aurence Hancock, United States Marine. Semper Fi, Sweetie."

It was a special thrill for me to act as a chapel. And to think, just a few months ago I was amusing myself with my own memories and trying to impress the few visitors who ambled through the Texas museum.

Just when I thought the evening was drawing to a near, I was transformed from a chapel into a museum. What an honor it was for me to have Colonel Ben Purcell gently lay an ancient case on my seats and open it, revealing authentic items he had salvaged from his five years as a POW. With spotlights and cameras rolling, he pointed to and told stories about each item in his case, including the clothes he wore out of the camp. He spoke to a spellbound crowd as the bewitching hour neared.

Wherever I was, as I watched the fans head back to their homes for the evenings, I held the terrifying belief that I would turn back into a rust bucket at the stroke of midnight. Fortunately, I was always my same new self when I arose each morning. But on this evening, after the crowd had long dispersed and I was in deep sleep amongst nothing but the sounds of the crickets and the flowing river, someone flicked on the spotlights jolting me awake. I half expected to find myself back in Texas until I saw Aurence tiptoeing toward me with a small bag of paints and paintbrushes. He was going to paint on my starboard door; I had heard them talking about it earlier. Aurence is a folk artist who paints Vietnam War scenes, and he had been asked to paint the POW emblem on my starboard side as well as other familiar icons that distinguish his art. I settled back into the moment as he went about the loving task of gently brushing my side with paint. It was a special time for both of us. As the whole world slept, two war relics connected. We spent a few surrealistic hours together, and I eventually drifted back into a deep sleep.

When I woke, there was the POW symbol, Aurence's trademarks: a White Dog, a fireball, and his signature tribute to a young Marine, Danny Dean McGee, who back in 1965 joined the Marines with Aurence. Danny never returned from Vietnam, and Aurence honors him in everything he paints by painting a squiggly that resembles a "D" with two hatch marks inside, both representing "Ds."

The crowd began to gather as the sun rose. I was still squinting myself awake as people walked by sipping cups of steaming coffee, saying their goodbyes to me as my flags were removed and I was prepared for the next leg of my journey. I was purring like a kitten at liftoff as the trees mercifully gave way to the whooshing of my powerful blades. My heart felt heavy as I pulled pitch. I did not want to leave this peaceful setting by the river, but there were more people to honor and more hearts to heal. I soon looked forward to my next stop and took solace that onboard sat not only Aurence and Colonel Ben Purcell, who rode to the next stop, but the spirit of Danny Dean McGee, symbol of all the young boys who never came home. As long as I fly, people will know Danny.

I made many more stops before my *Tour of Duty* ended in Angel Fire. My fairy tale did not end there, however, and I am now engaged in another tour that will end in a place of honor. "Where?" you ask. Well, you will hear about it when it happens. Come and see me. Just ask for 091. Danny and I will be waiting for you.

✈ By Patty Biegun
http://www.aurence.net
http://www.aurence.net/photog.htm

Patty Biegun is a freelance writer living with her Vietnam War folk artist husband, Larry Hancock, aka Aurence. They live a peaceful life on the banks of the

Chattahoochee River in northeast Georgia, with their six cats and Yellow Labrador. Biegun has written articles for daily newspapers, magazines, and veterans' publications and is an accomplished photojournalist. She is working on her first book, *To Honor Danny*, a book about Aurence and his high school friend Danny Dean McGee. The two friends entered the Marines on the Buddy Program and were separated after two weeks. Danny was killed shortly after arriving in Vietnam. Aurence was a Marine door gunner in Vietnam, 1966–1967, serving at Marble Mountain and Dong Ha. He received the Purple Heart for wounds received at the attack on Marble Mountain in July of 1967.

For more information on Huey 091 and the remarkable journey, visit *In the Shadow of the Blade*, http://www.intheshadowoftheblade.com

Read more about the 2002 adventures of Huey 091 by one of the crew, Bill McDonald, in his book, *A Spiritual Warrior's Journey*, http://www.lzangel.com/WarBook.htm

Read about Vietnam veteran Galen Foster in "In the End, It Was Always the Hueys," chapter 8, by Patty Biegun.

📖

CHAPTER 12

Everything I Need to Know

The aeroplane has unveiled for us the true face of the earth.
Antoine de Saint-Exupéry, 1900–1944

Winged Wisdom

ൟ If you are a pilot, smile at your crew chief;
it makes him think you know what you are doing.

Everything I Ever Needed to Know in Life, I Learned as a Helicopter Crewman in Vietnam

ൟ Once you are in the fight it is way too late to wonder if this is a good idea.

ൟ Helicopters are cool!

ൟ It is a fact that helicopter tail rotors are instinctively drawn toward trees, stumps, rocks, etc. While it may be possible to ward off this natural event some of the time, it cannot, despite the best efforts of the crew, always be prevented. It's just what they do.

ൟ *Never* get into a fight without more ammunition than the other guy.

ൟ The engine RPM and the rotor RPM must *both* be kept in the "green." Failure to heed this commandment can affect the morale of the crew.

ൟ A billfold in your hip pocket can numb your leg and be a real pain in the ass.

ൟ Cover your buddy, so he can be around to cover for you.

ൟ Letters from home are not always great.

117

- ❧ The madness of war can extract a heavy toll. Please have exact change.
- ❧ Share everything. Yes, even the Pound Cake.
- ❧ Decisions made by someone over your head will seldom be in your best interest.
- ❧ The terms "Protective Armor" and "Helicopter" are mutually exclusive.
- ❧ The farther away you are from your friends, the less likely it is that they can help you when you really need them most.
- ❧ Sometimes, being good and lucky still was not enough.
- ❧ There is always payback.
- ❧ Chicken Plates are not something you order in a restaurant.
- ❧ If everything is as clear as a bell and everything is going exactly as planned, you're about to be surprised.
- ❧ The BSR (Bang Stare Red) Theory states that the louder the sudden bang in the helicopter is, the quicker your eyes will be drawn to the gauges. The longer you stare at the gauges the less time it takes them to move from green to red.
- ❧ It does too get cold in Vietnam.
- ❧ No matter what you do, the bullet with your name on it will get you. So, too, can the ones addressed "To Whom It May Concern."
- ❧ Gravity: It may not be fair, but it is the law.
- ❧ If the rear echelon troops are really happy, the front line troops probably do not have what they need.
- ❧ If you are wearing body armor, they will probably miss that part.
- ❧ It hurts less to die with a uniform on, than to die in a hospital bed.
- ❧ Happiness is a belt-fed weapon.
- ❧ If something is not broken on your helicopter, it's about to.
- ❧ Eat when you can. Sleep when you can. Shit when you can. The next opportunity may not come around for a long time—if ever.
- ❧ "Combat Pay" is a flawed concept.
- ❧ Having all your body parts intact and functioning at the end of the day beats the alternative.
- ❧ Air superiority is *not* a luxury.
- ❧ If you are allergic to lead it is best to avoid a war zone.

- It is a bad thing to run out of airspeed, altitude, and ideas all at the same time.
- While the rest of the crew may be in the same predicament, it's usually the pilot's job to be the first to arrive at the scene of the crash.
- When you shoot your gun, clean it the first chance you get.
- Loud, sudden noises in a helicopter *will* get your undivided attention.
- Hot garrison chow is better than hot C-rations, which, in turn, are better than cold C-rations, which are better than no food at all. All of these, however, are preferable to cold rice balls even if they do have the little pieces of fish in them.
- NEVER FORGET!
- WHAT is often more important than WHY.
- Boxes of cookies from home must be shared.
- Girlfriends are fair game. Wives are not.
- Everybody's a hero…on the ground…in the club…after the fourth drink.
- There is no such thing as a small firefight.
- A free fire zone has nothing to do with economics.
- The farther you fly into the mountains, the louder the strange engine noises become.
- Medals are OK, but having your body and all your friends in one piece at the end of the day is better.
- Being shot hurts.
- "Pucker Factor" is the formal name of the equation that states the more hairy the situation is, the more of the seat cushion will be sucked up your butt. It can be expressed in its mathematical formula of S (suction) + H (height above ground) + I (interest in staying alive) + T (number of tracers coming your way). Thus the term "SHIT!" can also be used to denote a situation where a high Pucker Factor is being encountered.
- Thousands of Vietnam veterans earned medals for bravery every day. A few were even awarded.
- Running out of pedal, fore or aft cyclic, or collective are all bad ideas. Any combination of these can be deadly.
- Nomex is *not* fireproof.

- There is only one rule in war: When you win, you get to make up the rules.
- Living and dying can both hurt a lot.
- Do not wear underwear. It can cause crotch rot or be used as evidence against you.
- While a Super Bomb could be considered one of the four essential building blocks of life, powdered eggs cannot.
- C-4 can make a dull day fun.
- Of course you can drink out of a human skull! Duct tape over the eye sockets will keep it from leaking.
- Cocoa Powder is neither.
- There is no such thing as a fair fight—only ones where you win or lose.
- If you win the battle, you are entitled to the spoils. If you lose, you don't care.
- Nobody cares what you did yesterday or what you are going to do tomorrow. What is important is what you are doing *now* to solve our problem.
- If you have extra—share quickly.
- It's OK to take stuff off the body of a buddy, 'cause you know he would have wanted you to have it anyway.
- Always make sure someone has a P-38.
- A sucking chest wound may be God's way of telling you it's time to go home.
- Prayer may not help—but it can't hurt.
- Flying is better than walking. Walking is better than running. Running is better than crawling. All of these, however, are better than extraction by a Med-Evac even if it is, technically, a form of flying.
- If everyone does not come home, none of the rest of us can ever fully come home either.
- Do not fear the enemy, for your enemy can only take your life. It is far better that you fear the media, for they will steal your *honor*.
- The grunt is the true reason for the existence of the helicopter. Every helicopter flying in Vietnam had one real purpose—to help the grunt. It is unfortunate that many helicopters never had the opportunity to fulfill their one true mission in life, simply because someone forgot this fact.
- "You have the right to remain silent," is always excellent advice.

- ◌ If you have not been there and done that, you will probably not understand most of these.

- ✦ By Bobby L. McBride
  128th Assault Helicopter Company, crew chief
  Phu Loi, RVN March 1969–March 1970
  Reprinted with permission.

Many thanks to my fellow Vietnam helicopter flight crew member brothers who helped compile this list: J.C. Pennington, Lee Westbrook, Bob Blum, Ron Timberlake, and Darryl James ✦ Bobby McBride

📖

Rules to Live By

- ◌ Never yell whoa in a mudhole.
- ◌ Helicopters don't fly…they beat the air into submission.
- ◌ Helicopter Pilots do it on the backside of the power curve.
- ◌ The Shivering, shuttering, shaking, shithouse. (used to describe the CH-34, Choctaw Helicopter)
- ◌ It's not the fall that kills ya, it's the sudden stop.
- ◌ A gaggle of helos can soon turn into a cluster of metal.
- ◌ "Marble Tower, this is Dimmer, do you know where I'm at?"

- ✦ Contributed by Pat Kenny, Semper Fi
  HMM-364 Purple Foxes, http://www.hmm-364.org
  April 1970–April 1971, Vietnam, USMC, helicopter pilot
  Marble Mountain Air Facility, I Corps
  See Pat Kenny's comments on "Amazing Machines," chapter 6.

📖

CHAPTER 13

Helicopter History

You can't help but have the feeling
that there will come a future generation...
who will look at old pictures of helicopters and say,
"You've got to be kidding."

Harry Reasoner, 1923–1991

Winged Wisdom

෬ If you use mnemonics, you can memorize
large amounts of superfluous material.
෬ Don't try to memorize large amounts of important
information, write it on your kneeboard.
෬ Learn a little history about your job.
It will add to your wisdom.

Never Stop Improving on What You Have

The English word helicopter comes from the French who coined hélicoptère. They combined two Greek words, heliko and pteron. Heliko means spiral, and pteron means wing.

The first manned flight of a helicopter was November 13, 1907, by Frenchman Paul Cornu. Historians consider this the first free flight, not tethered to the ground, of a rotorcraft capable of vertical flight.

Cornu stayed suspended about a foot above the earth for only a few seconds on that first try, but this was sufficient to get his name in the history books. In

nt hovering attempts, Cornu managed to move slightly forward and
ut his machine lacked any real means of controlling the flight.

uis Charles Breguet designed a gyroplane that actually lifted off the ground
uple of months before Cornu. Four ground handlers, however, steadied his
raft. Breguet's achievement is noteworthy in the fact that it was the first time
at a rotary craft with a human inside had lifted successfully from the ground.

Cornu's achievement was only four years after the famous Wright brothers'
first airplane flight on December 17, 1903. The Wright brothers attempted to fly
helicopter models in 1878. History records state that the brothers agreed that
vertical flight was not possible, and they abandoned the idea to focus on fixed-
wing flight.

Long before the Wrights or Cornu dreamed of upward, backward, and side-
ways flight, Leonardo da Vinci was thinking of it in the 1480s. The famous
Italian artist left behind sketches for what he called a lifting screw or helical air
screw.

"I have discovered that a screw-shaped device such as this, if it is well-made
from starched linen, will rise in the air if turned quickly," said Da Vinci.

Although history records man's dreaming of vertical flight from as early as the
4th century in China, not much was done about it until the 1700s. It was a
Frenchman, J.P. Paucton, who added to Leonardo da Vinci's design with his idea
called the pterophore. He suggested another screw, a horizontal axis rotor, in
addition to the one that lifted in vertical flight. This second screw would allow
horizontal flight in any direction. After Paucton's idea of upward and horizontal
flight in 1768, two Frenchmen, M. Launoy and M. Bienvenu invented two
superimposed screws with feathers.

"The horizontal percussions of the air neutralize each other, and the vertical
percussions combine to raise the machine," they explained.

Inventors continued to crash and burn over the next century as their ideas and
flying contraptions added to the completion of the puzzle of vertical and horizontal flight.

Nearly 400 documented years in the making, the helicopter was now almost a
reality. The internal combustion engine in 1876 was the final touch needed to
complete the launching of this ingenious flying machine. This allowed it to be
light enough to carry its pilot, a necessity, and to achieve flight, the objective.
Next came the flying control problems.

Juan de la Cierva invented the autogiro in the 1920s. His invention was one of
the greatest contributions to the development of today's helicopter. He came up
with the idea of an angled hinge on the rotor hub that allows the blades to flap
freely up and down with rotation. This simple idea allows for stable flight as the
flexible blades adjust to the changing airflow caused by rotation.

A native Russian gets the final credit for the success of today's helic[...] Connecticut, on September 14, 1934, more than four centuries after Le[...] da Vinci's first drawings, Igor Sikorsky lifted his VS-300 helicopter o[...] ground.

The VS-300 had a four-cylinder, 75-horsepower air-cooled engine wit[...] power transmission. It had three blades on the main rotor and wheeled landi[...] gear. Igor Sikorsky eventually set a world record for helicopter endurance of on[...] hour, 32 minutes, and 26 seconds in the air.

Sikorsky and the other helicopter manufacturers that followed him adhered to the number one rule: Never stop improving on what you have.

The military was the first to jump on Sikorsky's "new" invention. They used a few helicopters in World War II. By the Korean War in the 1950s, hundreds were whop-whopping their way around the skies. They served mainly to aid in enemy observation and to move wounded soldiers.

With the invention of the turboshaft engine in the mid-1950s, Larry Bell, another manufacturer of helicopters, came out with his Huey model. It was lighter, bigger, and more powerful. During the Vietnam War, the versatile Huey moved soldiers into the battle zone, carried wounded, and easily landed in small clearings in the jungle.

The helicopter has proved itself useful in many more ways than just as a wartime airship. Its ability to land where airplanes cannot has made it popular for businesses as well as public services. Helicopter pilots also can fly at night, getting down to treetop level with bright spotlights, which makes the helicopter useful for police and search and rescue missions.

Medevac, ambulance helicopters, are often able to get to the scene of an accident and back to the hospital more quickly than a ground vehicle. Many large ships and offshore oil rigs use helicopters to bring people and supplies back and forth from shore. Furthermore, some remote areas have found the helicopter to be ideal for delivery of mail and supplies.

Passenger helicopter flights also have become quite commonplace. Since the helicopter does not need a runway, only a cleared area to land, it can be used in ways and places that a fixed-wing plane cannot.

This chapter is, of course, not a complete history of the helicopter. Over the centuries, numerous people contributed in small and large ways to what is today's helicopter. Rotary aircraft continue to change with innovative improvements and technological advancements.

✦ Reprinted from *KISS the Sky: Helicopter Tales.*

CHAPTER 14

Why Fly?

Why fly?
Simple. I'm not happy
unless there's some room
between me and the ground.

Richard Bach, 1936–present
A Gift of Wings

The Sky

Another year has passed me by
And no matter how hard I try
I never forget my love for the sky.

I can't figure it out, what's it all about
The autorotation that will make you shout
The joy in my heart and the wind in my face
The adrenaline rush that just took place.

Will I ever before I die
Give up my love for the sky?

To push a Huey to the edge
To drag its skids through the hedge
To sail so high through the billowing mist
Just to get an Angel's kiss.

Will I ever before I die
Give up my love for the sky?

To feel again the taste of steel
The tracers flying that make you squeal
Pulling triggers to the max
Shooting rockets, watching tachs.

Will I ever before I die
Give up my love for the sky?

I know what it means to live a lie
When I had to give up my love for the sky.

✈ By Ron Leonard
Diamondhead 085, 25th Aviation Battalion, 25th Infantry Division
March1968–April 1969, Cu Chi, Vietnam
http://25thaviation.org

📖

Winged Wisdom

ભ Getting paid for something you love to do
is the best feeling in the world.
ભ Thank God that you fly.

The Last Ride

For days the anticipation of the reunion of B Company 25th Aviation Battalion had been running through my head. It would be the first time many of us had seen each other in 33-plus years in Cu Chi, Vietnam. It would prove to be an emotional experience. One of healing, long-lost camaraderie, and laughter—a weekend to remember for a lifetime.

I had worked many thousands of hours to make this happen. The men of Diamondhead were brothers like no others I had met in my life. I needed to find them, to say goodbye before I was gone back to some pile of ashes perched on a shelf somewhere without ever having had the chance.

d fought a valiant war for an unappreciative America. We had risked our
 each other, some of us losing it. Maybe these upcoming few days were
 was spared. On October 4, 1968, I should have died in a midair collision
 r some reason was spared. Maybe this was why.

took it upon myself to give us what we were cheated out of, to somehow
ke it right for us, if only for a weekend. I spent more than a year locating first
e member then another until I had found about 250. We needed a reunion to
lp heal those wounds we had inside, the ones you can't see. The ones embedded
n your soul. The ones you dream about and wake up sweating and screaming
with. The ones you have no one to talk to about who really understands. Only
the camaraderie of Diamondhead could do that. We were a "Band of Brothers,"
and I would just have to band them together again one last time. Maybe none of
them would understand the importance of being with each other one more time
until it was over, but they would in the end understand.

We got no damn parade when we came home, only jeers and abuse. I would
give us the parade we needed, Our Parade, the one we never got when we came
home. We deserved it.

With the help of Paul Pelland, a Charleston resident and former Vietnam helicopter pilot, the details were worked out with the Citadel in Charleston, South
Carolina. We would be the guests of honor, or at least some of the guests of
honor, at their traditional Friday parade on April 12. That was accomplished and
everyone appreciated it. I saw the smiles. I saw hardened veterans starting to
soften and become, if just for a little while, the youth they once were. To me those
memories will always be priceless. Those mental images themselves had been
worth all the effort to make it happen.

I needed something else. I needed a helicopter. The common bond we all had
of the "Helicopter War" fought in a far away place called Vietnam. It would be
the glue that stuck the event together. It would be the catalyst of the rebonding
that would occur. I knew of a Diamondhead OH-6 that was being restored in
California. I contacted the owners, and it wouldn't be ready in time, maybe for
Reunion Phase II in Phoenix in June, so I would just have to settle for any old
Huey. I guess that would be better than no helicopter at all.

Out of the blue, Steve Lindley, a sergeant with the Anderson County Sheriffs
Department, contacted me and wanted to know if he could bring one of our old
ships to the reunion. I nearly had a heart attack. My prayers had been answered.
It was not just any Huey, it was 961, an old bird we all had intimate knowledge
of. It was our old Smoke Ship. Innumerable medals had been earned in that ship.
It still had the bullet holes of honor and battle scars it acquired with us in
Vietnam. It had rescued LRRP (long-range reconnaissance patrol) teams from
certain death, it had medevaced dying soldiers to the 12th Evacuation Hospital

who otherwise wouldn't have survived, and it had rescued downed ⌐
crews. Yes, she was a hero herself. She had but one more Diamondhead ⌐
to accomplish, "Our Last Ride," the ride that would make us whole ag⌐
ride that would bring one chapter in our lives to an end.

As Saturday morning arrived, the weather was clearing in Charleston,⌐
there was a 200-foot ceiling in Greenville, South Carolina. 961's departure ⌐
been delayed. God could not let this happen. This final chapter had to be play⌐
out in its entirety. It could not end like our war in Vietnam, half done. Finally, ⌐
1 p.m. the call came on the cell phone that the weather had cleared, and they⌐
were inbound and would arrive in an hour. As time ticked away the anticipation ⌐
grew.

I had for months kept a secret. I had told them the aircraft was flying in, but I
had failed to tell them, the old crew members, they would get to go flying. In case
something went wrong, I didn't want myself or the crew members to bear the dis-
appointment of it not happening.

In the distance we could hear that all familiar Wop, Wop, Wop that only a
Huey makes. It brought cold chills up my spine. Very faintly at first, but as she
got closer the crescendo got louder and louder until it rattled the windows of the
hotel as she settled to the grass in the vacant lot behind the Holiday Inn. As I
surveyed the crowd, I found Jack Mosley and Poncho Salazar hugging each other,
and so many smiles you couldn't count them all. I, too, was smiling; my little plan
was coming together, and I still had the secret they didn't know safely secured in
my head.

As her engine shut down, and as her blades whistled in the afternoon breeze
slowly coming to a stop, her old pilots and crew members mobbed her. They were
climbing on her like it was yesterday to check out all the bullet holes and scars of
honor she had earned so long ago. Poncho Salazar, her old crew chief, and Jack
Mosley, her old gunner, climbed up in the gunners' wells which had been home
so many years ago. Charlie Burnett, once her gunner, was also checking out the
intimate portions of the old girl he knew. I got out the camera to capture those
personal memories forever.

We had five pilots on hand who had flown this old bird on many combat
missions, and they took their places in the pilots' seats and made that last picture.
It was beautiful and brought back oh so many memories from that distant land
we all knew so well.

While everyone was taking pictures and reminiscing the past adventures of
this old bird, I walked over to Steve Lindley and thanked him for bringing her,
and presented him and the crew that flew her to Charleston with a Diamondhead
patch. That would link the past with the future. Wherever they would go, something of us would be with them. We discussed "The Last Ride," which was

nd would occur. Still, the secret of what would soon occur was secure in

First Sergeant Davison took up a collection, and we sent the Sheriffs
rtment off to lunch in style. Upon their return from lunch, Sgt. Lindley
ted at Jack Mosley, Poncho Salazar, Chuck Burnett, and myself to get in the
k where we quickly staked out our favorite spots. Bob Segers was assigned the
t seat. Everyone buckled in but me, the seat belt was refusing to work; I don't
are how far I sucked in my not-so-skinny old gut. Poncho was sitting in the floor
with his feet dangling out the right side, Chuck Burnett in the passenger seat next
to the door, Jack Mosley in the gunner's well on the left side, and myself still
struggling with the seat belt in the right side gunner's well.

Sgt. Lindley hit the starter switch and the old girl responded immediately—
the whine of the starter generators kicking in, the tic-tic-tic of the igniters searching for fuel, the whoosh of ignition, the blades slowly starting to spin as they
searched for 6,000 RPM, the singing of the blades as they cut through the afternoon air, the pungent odor of burnt JP-4 in the air. It brought back the memories
of those late night missions so long ago. I remembered the good times and the
bad times.

In my mind I could still hear the pilots of yesteryear, "Cu Chi tower, Cu Chi
tower, this is Diamondhead 961 on the Beach, scramble."

And the towers reply, "Roger, Diamondhead, you're clear south on the active."

Then the beeping of the engine up to 6,600 RPM as the blades beat the air
into submission. Yes, those were the days.

We lifted off and could feel the lightness on the skids, which put a huge smile
on my face. Poncho's and my eyes met, nothing but smiles, no words were neces-
sary. Sgt. Lindley brought her up to a 20-foot hover, tipped the nose over, and we
were off and quickly up to 800 feet, and turning right up the Cooper River. Below
I could make out a yacht, if it were only a Sampan it would have been heaven. It
seemed a little odd to not have an M-60 machine gun in the mount in front of me,
but that was OK. In my old age I would probably hurt myself with one. We swung
out over the trees and dropped it down and buzzed along just off their tops, and I
caught myself looking for bunkers and spider holes. Such memories.

Over the intercom I heard Sgt. Lindley ask Bob Segers if he wanted to fly her.
I agree with Bob, that was the dumbest question of all time. In about two seconds
Bob was right at home, just like he had done so many times before. We flew on
for five or 10 minutes. We encountered a little turbulence and the blades popped
as it clawed at the air. It was like music to my ears.

Soon we were headed back to the LZ (landing zone), but Bob just had to do
something fun, no straight-in approach, no sir, not today. A tight 360 over the
Hampton Inn across the street at 500 feet almost standing her on her side was the

call of the hour. That brought a group cheer from all of us in the back
that lady in the swimming pool flashed us with her bathing suit top. I lob
a go-around to make sure but was overruled. I had flashed back to the old
tion out of Dau Tieng and the French lady we would sneak up on in the
there occasionally. Yeah, those were the times.

It had been 15 minutes of heaven. Fifteen minutes that would put to rest
lifetime of pain and a closing of a chapter in our lives. It was also the beginning
a new era, a new chapter in our lives of new friendships, and continuations of old
ones, that hopefully would grow and continue on far into the future. It had been
"The Last Ride," but what a ride.

✛ By Ron Leonard
    Diamondhead 085, 25th Aviation Battalion, 25th Infantry Division
    March 1968–April 1969, Cu Chi, Vietnam
    http://25thaviation.org

    See Ron Leonard's story "The Midair," chapter 6.

AFTERWORD
(POSTFLIGHT)

Winged Wisdom

ભ Never assume someone else has done a preflight for you.

ભ Never assume that yesterday's preflight is still good for today.

ભ Always do a postflight.

ભ If you don't know the nomenclature of something, draw a picture.

ભ Don't pretend to be smarter than you are.

ભ You will perform a task exactly as you rehearsed it.

ભ Know what the little lights on the dash mean.

ભ Ask questions of those who have more experience than you do.

ભ Don't brag to those you have more experience than.

📖

Much of what I need to know for everyday living, I learned from flying Huey helicopters for the U.S. Army. Even though these thoughts apply literally to flying, they have become my philosophies for life as well. Throughout the book, *Winged Wisdom*, are excerpts from my book *KISS the Sky: Helicopter Tales*.

ભ Remember to kiss (KIS),
Keep It Simple;
life has enough rules.

Jan Hornung
http://www.geocities.com/vietnamfront

ABOUT JAN HORNUNG

http://www.geocities.com/vietnamfront

J an Hornung served her country as a UH-1 helicopter pilot in the 1980s. After leaving the U.S. Army, she began a new career as a newspaper writer/editor and later as an instructor for college-level English composition. She holds a bachelor's degree from Texas A&M University and a master's in aeronautical science from Embry-Riddle Aeronautical University.

She has earned several writing awards, and in addition to *Spinning Tails: Helicopter Stories,* she has published four other books:

∝ *This Is The Truth, As Far As I Know: I Could Be Wrong*

∝ *If A Frog Had Wings* (no longer in print)

∝ *KISS the Sky: Helicopter Tales*

∝ *Angels in Vietnam: Women Who Served*

To contact writers and poets featured in the book, do so via their web sites listed or through Jan Hornung's e-mail listed at her web site: http://www.geocities.com/vietnamfront

BOOKS BY JAN HORNUNG

www.geocities.com/vietnamfront

Angels in Vietnam: Women Who Served

*A*ngels in Vietnam is a collection of stories, poems, and pictures by and about the women who served in Vietnam during the war. For more than a decade, from the early 1960s, more than 11,000 women from America, New Zealand, and Australia went to Vietnam as nurses, American Red Cross workers, physical therapists, entertainers, librarians, and more. Cry, laugh, and share a year in Vietnam with the *Angels in Vietnam: Women Who Served.*

Ride along in a UH-1 Huey on a Christmas Day mission of the heart with Army pilots and American Red Cross Donut Dollies in Vietnam in 1969. Meet Gary's angel, a physical therapist whom a wounded soldier found nearly 35 years later so that he could tell her, "Thank you." Take a trip back to the war with a Donut Dolly when she finds her true love, a soldier fighting in Nam. Experience the war through a nurse's eyes. Read about the Australians and the New Zealanders who served in the Vietnam War. Find out why male Vietnam veterans think the women who nursed, comforted, entertained, or just talked with them were the *Angels in Vietnam.*

This is the Truth as Far as I Know, I Could Be Wrong

*T*his is a knee-slapping, nose-snorting, hilariously funny book of short stories about life in the South, life in the military, and life of a southerner in Europe by the award-winning humor columnist Jan Hornung.

Go to the Bubba Fest, learn about the wurst of all wieners, and do the Doggy Dance of Joy. Find out if you have vacaphobia, how to tell if you're nekkid, and lessons on marriage from your dog and helicopters. You'll be busier than a mosquito in a nudist colony reading short stories such as "Armadillo Wine," "Eat Crackers and Whistle Your National Anthem," "My Dog is Planet Uranus," and "Hoodoo, Doorknobs, and Automobiles."

As Jan says, "Everything in this book is *The Truth as Far as I Know, I Co Wrong.*"

📖

KISS the Sky: Helicopter Tales

Former military pilot Jan Hornung takes you flying in this rib-tickling, rolling-in-the-aisles hilariously funny book of short stories about flying helicopters in the Army.

Whether you fly fixed-wing or rotary-wing, or you know someone's second cousin twice removed who flies kites, this collection of short stories will amuse pilots and pilot wannabes of all ages.

Included in this book is a history of helicopter flight, women in aviation, and a lesson on how helicopters fly.

📖

BIBLIOGRAPHY

or "Flight Facts" and history used throughout this book, thanks to the following: The Vietnam Helicopter Pilots Association, http://www.vhpa.org; ll McDonald's *The Vietnam Experience*, http://www. vietnamexp.com; The ietnam Helicopter Flight Crew Network, http://www.vhfcn.org; The Dustoff ssociation, http://www.dustoff.org; Australia and New Zealand Army Corps, ANZAC, history, archived by the Australian National Library, http://www.anzacday.org.au; *Get the Bloody Job Done* by Steve Eather; No. 9 Squadron, RAAF in Vietnam, http://airwarvietnam.com/raafno9.htm; *Air War Vietnam*, airwarvietnam.com; *Helicopter History*, www.helis.com; the Veterans' Administration; *Military Helicopters* by Bill Gunston; *The Illustrated History of Helicopters* by Michael Heatley; and *The Helicopters, The Epic of Flight*, Time-Life Books.

📖